CONFESSIONS OF AN UNMANAGER

TEN STEPS TO JUMP START COMPANY PERFORMANCE BY GETTING OTHERS TO ACCEPT ACCOUNTABILITY

ALSO BY THE AUTHORS

BURIED ALIVE!
DIGGING OUT OF A MANAGEMENT DUMPSTER

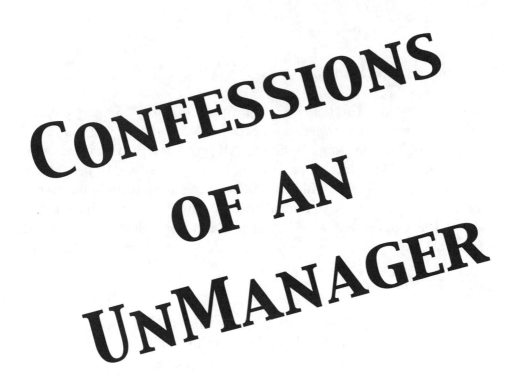

CONFESSIONS OF AN UNMANAGER

TEN STEPS TO JUMP START COMPANY PERFORMANCE BY GETTING OTHERS TO ACCEPT ACCOUNTABILITY

BY
DEBRA BOGGAN & ANNA VERSTEEG

THE OAKLEA PRESS

RICHMOND, VIRGINIA

First Trade Paperback Edition

Confessions of an UnManager: Ten Steps to Jump Start Company Performance by Getting Others to Accept Responsibility © 1997 and 2004 by Debra Boggan and Anna VerSteeg. All rights reserved. Printed in the United States of America. No part of this book may be used or reproduced in any manner whatsoever without written permission except in the case of brief quotations embodied in critical articles and reviews. For information address The Oaklea Press, 6912 Three Chopt Road, Suite B, Richmond, Virginia 23226.

ISBN 1-892538-14-8

If your bookseller does not have this book in stock,
it can be ordered directly from the publisher.
Contact us for information about discounts
on quantity purchases.

The Oaklea Press
6912 Three Chopt Road, Suite B
Richmond, Virginia 23226

Voice: 1-800-295-4066
Facsimile: 1-804-281-5686
Email: Info@OakleaPress.com

This book can be purchased online at

http://www.LeanTransformation.com

PREFACE

This is a fictionalized account of an odyssey we undertook to change the way we do business. As the general plant manager and operations manager of the Northern Telecom Customer Service Repair Center in Morrisville, North Carolina, we learned that the leadership processes and techniques we had grown comfortable and successful with simply weren't good enough anymore to meet our business objectives. We decided we needed to adopt a new way, the team way of doing business.

Originally, Northern Telecom was structured in a traditional hierarchical manner. Under the guise of change, Northern Telecom's employees formed organizational teams, which then assumed daily business accountability. Specifically, employee teams tracked and implemented business objectives, monitored budgets, and drove effective development, cultural support, and usage of company policies, as well as team processes and procedures. We, as leaders, played the critical role in this process of establishing total business accountability at every level and area of the organization.

The results were staggering, involving quantum improvements of up to 120 percent in bottom-line revenue, quality, and customer service. In addition, we were honored to have been featured on the *CBS Evening News* in 1991.

It is now a few years later and we wanted to share with you some of the important techniques we've learned. We created this novel in an effort to take you through many of the processes involved in transforming a traditional business environment into one based on the principles of Unmanagement. Please take note — this book is entirely fictional and any resemblance to real people, living or dead, is entirely coincidental. Besides, we suspect many of the characters in this book are universal and, therefore, bound to sound like someone you know.

Companies have been striking out with self-directed teams, high-performance teams, empowerment, steering committees, design committees, quality circles, project teams and reengineering. It is time to put business back into the ball game. There exists a universe of untapped resources in the average workplace. It is time for business leadership to acknowledge this and take a committed stand in their organizations toward focused business teams. Project teams, task forces, and steering committees, though positive trends, are simply the "tip of the iceberg."

We have been there, done that, and proven that it can work. It is our goal that our story helps you to learn "how."

This book is dedicated with sincerest fondness and appreciation to the people who showed us "how" — the employees of the Northern Telecom Customer Service Repair Center in Morrisville, North Carolina. Thank you for the knowledge and the lessons that have developed us to our fullest potential.

Good luck on your journey and keep the faith!

CONTENTS

Preface iii

About the Authors vii

1   All Shook Up 1

2   Two Different Worlds 7

3   The Calm Before the Storm 15

4   Through the Looking Glass 21

5   Major Disappointments 29

6   Sir Isaac Trisha 33

7   We're Not in Kansas Anymore 37

8   Great Expectations 49

9   Seeing Is Believing 59

10   Leadership 63

11   The Death of a Primate 73

12   Process, Teams, and "Ergonomic" Dave 81

13   Trisha and the Lion Tamer 89

14   Feels Like Team Spirit 95

15   "Operation Egghead" 103

16   Trouble in Paradise 115

17   The First Big Payoff 123

18   The Ratings Game 133

19   High Quality and "Franklin's Folly" 145

20   Customer Service Was Never Like this 155

21   "Operation Piggyback" and the Company of the Future 165

22   Moments of Truth 179

23   Good Times and a Parting Principle 187

24   Pass It On 191

ABOUT THE AUTHORS

Debra Boggan and Anna VerSteeg, as general plant manager and operations manager at the Northern Telecom Customer Service Repair Center in Morrisville, North Carolina, learned that the leadership processes and techniques they had grown comfortable with no longer served to meet the company's business objectives.

In response they developed the principles of "Unmanagement." Employees formed teams that monitored budgets, implemented business objectives, and played major roles in developing processes, procedures, company policy, and cultural support. As leaders, Boggan and VerSteeg served to drive the process that led to establishing business accountability at every level and area in the organization.

Boggan and VerSteeg in 1991 established Creative Solutions Incorporated as a vehicle for spreading the word of Unmanagement and teaching companies how to create and sustain a business-focused, work-team culture. Their proven implementation processes and training programs have produced measurable, significant bottom-line improvements in companies in the U.S. and Canada, spanning service, government, manufacturing, and military organizations.

Chapter One

ALL SHOOK UP

I decided to sit down and write about what really happened here at FineFax, Inc., since lately, the stories in some of the newspapers and magazines have been getting a little too carried away. While it is true that we discovered an unusually effective management style that we called "Unmanagement," it's a bit much, for my tastes anyway, to have to read that we achieved "a revolutionary management breakthrough of epic proportions." And while it is also true that Unmanagement caused the plant's profits to increase by more than 50 percent because we reduced operating costs and finished goods inventories, cut quality defects and customer complaints, and improved productivity, it makes me edgy when reporters start calling our results "spectacular corporate pyrotechnics." It's just not my style. You know what I mean?

Still, to be perfectly honest, I probably could've lived with an occasional overblown adjective. After all, it's a high-class problem, right? What really pushed me over the edge was an article in the local *Clarion News* that claimed at one point that "the principles of Unmanagement that powered the FineFax success were conceived and executed by Trisha Morris, the plant's resident management genius." Now that one really bothered me, and right then I promised myself that I would set the record straight.

First, I'm no more a genius than I am Madonna, although once I did do a respectable imitation of her; I'll tell you about that later. Second, and contrary to what the *Clarion* article suggests, I did not do everything myself — there were some 400 people involved. Nor did the whole Unmanagement idea just pop right out of my head, all put together and ready to go. As I just said — everybody in the plant worked on it, a bunch of basically ordinary people all stumbling forward together.

To me it's important that you know the truth because I'm hoping you'll try Unmanagement for yourself. That wouldn't be likely if you thought you had to be a rocket scientist to do it.

So with that said, let me tell you what happened at FineFax.

Actually, the experience that eventually triggered Unmanagement here at the plant kind of sneaked up on me several years before I ever got to FineFax. I almost missed the significance of the event. I suppose I shouldn't be too hard on myself though, because back then I was far from being an unmanager, and I'm lucky I noticed anything at all.

At the time, I was operations manager of Modular Consoles, a small plant owned by Comlinks, Inc., a large corporation well known in world markets as a manufacturer of sophisticated telecommunications equipment. Modular Consoles assembled, wired, and tested telephone switchboards used by communication-intensive organizations, such as police departments and trucking companies. I had been working there for nearly eight years.

I had never taken any management courses in school, so when the time came for my first supervisory assignments at Modular, I simply decided to follow my natural inclinations. I had always enjoyed working with groups of people, actually getting involved in the work myself, and I never had any problem making friends. Basically, I felt that if all the people knew what had to be done, they could usually figure out the best way to do it on their own. This approach seemed to work just fine until it was pointed out to me in various subtle and not-so-subtle ways that, if I ever expected to further my management career, I would have to cultivate an entirely different persona. Other managers explained that I had to put some distance between me and the employees so I could become an all-knowing, authority-type figure. Employees, I was told, really don't possess much initiative or self-reliance, and they need continuous supervision, direction, and sometimes even outright intimidation. These ideas put me in a tough spot. A lot of it sounded nuts, but I was young and impressionable in those days. I was also a woman in management and did not want to appear any more conspicuous than I already was.

That's how I was recruited to an approach to management that is now called "command and control," a heavy-handed style inspired by the military services that is still widely used throughout business. Soon I was commanding and controlling with the best of them. Employees followed my orders; Trisha's orders were not negotiable. Before long, I accepted "command and control" as the natural and best method of running a business. I guess if you perpetuate tradition long enough, after a while you find yourself believing in it. As a result, I overlooked the fact that this approach often caused me to manage in ways that were both inappropriate and regrettable. Until the Brandt incident.

The whole thing started with a call that had come in early on a Friday evening. The plant, which ran only one shift at the time, had already closed. But Carlton Anderson, the plant's customer service representative, had decided to stay late to weed out his files. That's when a call came in from Fred Wilkins, the owner of a small, but busy, regional trucking firm and one of Anderson's best customers. He was in a panic. A wild electrical storm had just spiked the company's electrical system and had literally fried its office switchboard, along with a few other high-tech devices. Wilkins had to have another switchboard in place by the start of business Monday morning and asked if Anderson could please help him out. Anderson said he would see what could be done and would call Wilkins back, if not that night then by Saturday morning.

Anderson was not happy as he wandered out onto the production floor to reflect on his predicament. He knew he would have to disappoint Wilkins, but he simply had not wanted to tell him that outright during that call. Truth was, Modular Consoles had not yet developed a system that could respond to an emergency like Wilkins'. It was a weekend, the plant was closed, and that was that. Anderson was so preoccupied with his own thoughts that he nearly ran over Donald Brandt, who was coming out of the men's locker room. Brandt had returned to the plant to pick up a pair of high-tops that he had forgotten and that he now needed to play basketball. After they laughed about the near-collision, Anderson told Brandt his story and said it was too bad he couldn't help Wilkins because he knew the man and he liked him a lot.

Brandt thought about what he'd just heard for a moment and said, "Well, maybe there is a way to do it. Let me make a few calls. Can I get you at home tonight? It might be late."

"No problem," Anderson said. "Call anytime on this one."

Brandt called around 11:30 that night. "Good news," he said. "We put together a little pick-up team of selected all-stars from the production line who will solve your problem, Carlton. I will do the assembly work, Phil Klein will do the wiring, Alice Chapman will do the testing, and you, Carlton, will do the shipping. We'll meet you at the plant tomorrow morning, but I promised everybody it would be early so we'd have the rest of the day to ourselves."

"Oh, man, I can't let you do that," said Carlton. "I mean it's your day off."

"Carlton, do you want to help this guy or not?"

"Well, yeah, of course."

"Okay, then, quit complaining and meet us at the plant in the morning."

Brandt's pick-up team was a great success. They finished work on the console in under three hours. Anderson boxed the switchboard and had it ready when Federal Express arrived. When he called Wilkins that same morning, he was able to say that not only could he help him, but that the switchboard was already on its way. Wilkins, in turn, was practically delirious with gratitude.

On Monday morning, news of the team's weekend activities quickly spread through the plant. Brandt and his crew were all treated like champions. Not surprisingly, then, when I called the team into my office, they were sure their accomplishment was about to be acknowledged and praised officially. So they were stunned by what actually happened, and I don't blame them. It makes me wince to even tell the story; I can only do it because I'm not that way anymore.

"I understand that you all were in here working on Saturday," I said. "While I admire your industry, I have to tell you that you put in overtime without authorization, and I can't tolerate that. According to company policy, unauthorized overtime is subject to disciplinary action."

Then I launched into this monologue about the importance of following company policy in general, something about how policy added structure and a sense of direction to a business, and how could any business expect to succeed unless everybody followed the same direction, and on and on. The team sat there for a while listening slack-jawed while I rambled on. And do you know what? Never once did I mention their extraordinary customer service. As I said, it makes me wince. After I was done, they all filed out of the office and went back to their jobs. Brandt stopped at the door for a second, though, and said, "We never intended to put in for overtime."

"You didn't?" I replied, dumbfounded. "You mean you didn't do it for the money?"

"That's right," Brandt said, "We did it because Carlton needed help."

Maybe it was the utter simplicity of his parting remark, or maybe my time had come to have some kind, any kind, of revelation. Who knows? I can tell you, though, Brandt's remark shook me up. After eight years of Modular Consoles' "boot-camp" management conditioning, I now saw the first faint possibility of a much different and better relationship between managers and employees. I felt like a traveler who, well into a long and important journey, has just been told that she had been walking for years in the wrong direction. Suddenly, three hours of overtime did not seem so important anymore, nor did command and control seem to be the best way to run a business. "What's wrong with this picture?" I kept thinking. "Have I been missing something here?" My path toward Unmanagement had begun.

Chapter Two

TWO DIFFERENT WORLDS

In the children's story "The Emperor's New Clothes," two fast-talking swindlers posing as weavers convince the emperor that they can fashion a new suit of clothes for him that will make him the wonder of all his subjects. What's more, they say, it will be a magical suit of clothes because it will be invisible to anyone who is incompetent or stupid. Of course, the crafty swindlers have no intention of ever making a real suit; they are certain the foibles of human nature will protect their scam. Sure enough, when the emperor and his ministers come to see the imaginary suit as it is being created on the empty loom, they all praise its patterns and colors rather than risk their reputations. Later, the emperor even wears the new suit in a parade through his kingdom. As the emperor passes by, his subjects, who have already heard about the wondrous, magical garment, eagerly agree with one another that, yes, indeed, it is truly wondrous — see the bright color, the flowing cape, the fine stitching. Then a young boy in the crowd, not knowing any better, loudly asks his parents why the emperor isn't wearing any clothes. For a moment there is stunned silence. Then everyone is properly horrified because the truth can no longer be hidden.

I remembered this story because Brandt had roughly the same effect on me as the kid had on the emperor and his subjects. The emperor wasn't really wearing any magical clothes and, in effect, my management philosophy wasn't either. The employees on Brandt's pick-up team certainly didn't need continuous supervision as they were supposed to, nor did they lack for resourcefulness or initiative. Like the emperor's ministers and his subjects at the parade, the other managers and I had simply talked ourselves into believing something that wasn't true. Worse still, we had done such a good job at it that we thought our command-and-control method of managing was appropriate. After all, didn't our approach bring managers and employees together so they could get the work out? True, maybe we did have to use a little fear and intimidation to do it but, hey, that was only natural and, besides, employees appreciated a clear sense of direction. Then, whoops, along comes Brandt to blurt out that command and control really isn't wearing any clothes. And now what was I supposed to do?

At least one thing was clear. I got Brandt's team back together and told them they had done great work. Then, I got them overtime pay anyway and put a memo on the bulletin boards around the plant to officially recognize their accomplishment. But after that I really didn't know what to do. It started me thinking though. It was a gradual process over the next year or so, but after a while I actually got an insight or two.

My traditional management style wasn't the way things were meant to be at all. In fact, when I reevaluated my own experiences honestly enough, I could see that instead of bringing managers and employees together, it actually drove them farther apart. And following that line of reasoning a little farther, I decided I had discovered the headwaters of what must be the major problem in corporate America — namely, this great yawning chasm between how companies treat managers and how they treat employees. A lot of executives go around fretting over foreign competition, raw materials costs, unreliable vendors, and all kinds of things, but that's like worrying about the deck chairs on the *Titanic* compared to the Great Divide I'm talking about. Managers and employees may seem to be working in the same company, but they're really living in two different worlds.

On a clear day, I'm sure you can look at your own factory or office and see the Great Divide with no trouble at all. On one side are what I call the "Misguided Managers." They come in all shapes and sizes, each with his or her own misinformed notion of what it means to manage people. Some believe they have to control everything. They're trained to be assertive, aggressive, and even intimidating. And they're scared to death and completely stressed out that they'll overlook something. They just can't make a mistake, and God forbid, should they ever screw up, they'll have to admit it to someone.

Some believe they shouldn't waste their time talking to employees in a casual, personal manner. Associating with employees in anything other than a "managerial capacity" means they might not be keeping their eye on the brass ring. They stick to only other like-minded managers, slightly distanced from the rest of the staff, unless they are in the process of "managing" them.

Many of these managers are almost entirely focused on making their production numbers at all costs. They have a very short-term point of view and think in terms of quarterly results rather than long-term planning. Because they are so short-term oriented and they believe themselves responsible for virtually everything, misguided managers are also very reactive. They run around putting out fires all day and have a hard time freeing themselves to become proactive and anticipate the future.

Finally, most managers are treated like some elite ruling class. They're the only ones given the supposedly "confidential" numbers about the company's overall performance; they're given seminars and training in a wide variety of skills beyond their immediate job focus, such as hiring practices and negotiating; and for the stress they endure, they're given incredible salaries and bonuses, comfortable offices, and company cars — to name only a few of the perks.

Now, way over on the other side of the gap, you have the Employee Robots. Generally, the Employee Robots are extremely frustrated. Their jobs are structured so that they can only do one particular job, and only that job, all day. Most aren't taught any skills beyond those they need for the job. They're not given any information about how their company is doing in general. They're not given any additional responsibility or accountability beyond their immediate job, and even then their responsibility is limited because a separate quality inspection department usually checks their work. So, in a sense, these Employee Robots are not even responsible for their own work.

The employees' spirit of innovation and risk-taking was killed off long ago. Usually, new employees will arrive, brimming with possibilities. Excited at the opportunity to help out the company and be of value to their employer, they'll offer suggestions with the best of intentions. Then, the boom is dropped. Their suggestions are either ignored by their supervisors, or worse still, they're told these suggestions will be taken under advisement, and then nothing is done. That is why they have trained themselves not to comment on all the things around them that could be improved. They have seen so many productivity circles and supposedly miraculous "programs of the month" fizzle out that they've resigned themselves to the belief that corporate America will never do anything but abuse them.

So their whole outlook is, "This is where I work; this is not where I care to be. I'm wearing 'golden handcuffs,' and the only reason I'm here is money. I just put in my eight hours and go home. I don't want to help this company out; I don't want to give them any ideas." Most employees work within their little self-defined squares and do exactly as they are told and no more — like robots.

Let's not forget about the more subtle forms of discrimination between the managers and employees that may not be as obvious as offices and cars, but are nonetheless just as damaging and probably more so. These are the differences in expectations and standards. Clearly, what is expected of a person in a corporation varies according to who the person is and what that person does. If, for example, an employee makes a report to the chief executive officer of the company, he, like a great many CEOs, would not hold the employee to the same high standards governing effective presentations as he would a manager. The employee will take this to mean that he

Traditional Corporate Culture

MISGUIDED MANAGERS	THE GAP	EMPLOYEE ROBOTS
• All Knowing • Discriminatory Training • Total Accountability • Reactionary • Stress		• No Training Beyond Job • No Accountability • No Clear Direction • No Participation • No Ownership

or she is somehow a second-class citizen within the company, and the results are disastrous. The employee will not feel that his or her interests have anything to do with those of the company and, consequently, will not feel obliged to help the company succeed beyond the demands of routine assignments. There should be only one level of expectation for everyone, but instead the different expectations mean

1. unequal sense of ownership

2. unequal commitment.

The Territorial Imperative
TRADITIONAL MANUFACTURING ORGANIZATION

MATERIALS	DIRECT LABOR	SUPERVISOR	SALES/ MARKETING
• Expediting • Scheduling • Short-Term Planning • Inventory Control • Limited Production Knowledge	• Followers • Skill Expertise Only • Separate Inspection • Self-Focus	• Dictator • Reactive • Total Number/ Budget Control • Minimal Interpersonal Training	• Selling • Competitive Analysis • Forecasting

QUALITY	HUMAN RESOURCES	ACCOUNTING	ENGINEERING	CUSTOMER SERVICE
• Calculating Numbers • Presenting Data • Auditing Process	• Benefits • Procedures • Disciplinary Actions	• Budgets • Closing • Financials	• Process Design • Capacity Analysis • Standards • Approval Control	• Customer Complaints • Customer Response

At first I worried that maybe Modular Consoles was a rare duck, kind of uniquely screwed up, but I knew that couldn't be true. In eight years, I had visited other companies, and I also dropped in on vendors and sub-contractors whenever I could. The simple fact is that too many corporations have an environment, a "corporate culture," that keeps managers and employees apart by a wide distance.

And because of the mindset of employees and managers, most traditional corporations tend to arrange themselves into separate internal fiefdoms, each one aggressively guarded by its specific inhabitants.

Cooperative, integrated decision making in this dangerous landscape is hard to find. The company's leaders assume total responsibility for everything they can get their hands on. They have a "fix-it" mentality. They're reactive, stressed out, isolated, and tightly focused on controlling their production numbers at all costs.

The employees, that is, the company's direct labor, are the robot-followers with one-skill expertise whose work is watched by a separate inspection organization. They're not really involved in the company; they're not really concerned about the output; and they're not really concerned about quality because someone else is inspecting it. They care only about their one specific job.

The supervisors are very dictatorial and highly reactive because they don't have time to be proactive. They're running around watching and dictating and making sure that every single thing is going right. They have total numbers and budget control, and they have minimal interpersonal skills training. They're there to make sure that other people do work. They usually are not expected, and have not been trained, to motivate and teach employees.

The engineering department is very process design–oriented. They do all capacity analysis, write all standard operating procedures, and have total approval control; that is, they don't have to go to the supervisors, the employees, or anybody else for approval. Normally, they keep churning out their technical procedures and change processes without interfacing with anyone else.

The materials department expedites, runs around, and tries to make sure that the product gets out. They're doing all the scheduling, but it is very short-term scheduling because they, too, spend so much time simply reacting that they have little time left for forward planning. They're supposed to focus on production, but their actual knowledge of the production process is extremely limited. All they're really trying to do is control their inventory.

Of course, my background is in manufacturing, but I'm willing to bet that you would find the same conditions in service businesses. And even though there will probably be individual differences from business to business, the outcome would most likely be the same anyway. The extreme territorial focus creates an environment with little or no integration or communication, no shared knowledge, and no flexibility. And worst of all, even though all these people are supposed to be working toward one aim and supporting the product, they often end up with entirely different objectives and goals. Instead of harmony, they're actually fighting against each other and the overall objective of the company because they are all so concerned with controlling their own little fiefdoms. What follows is a good case in point.

The Curious Yet Instructive Tale of
Dave Polanski, the Engineer

One day, without telling anyone, Dave, a test engineer, went out into the plant and removed a piece of test equipment from one of the production lines, an action that changed the work flow on that particular line. The next day when the employees came to work, they were confused and upset that their normal routine had been undone. "Why is it gone?" they asked. "What happened to it? What's going to take its place?"

Later, I caught up with Dave. "Dave," I said, "please don't do that anymore unless you tell people first what you're going to do and why, so they can learn and have a chance to tell you what they think. People don't like surprises. After all, this is their work environment."

Two hours later, Dave came to see me, waving his job description that listed his official job responsibilities. "Nowhere on this piece of paper," Dave said indignantly, "does it say that I have to talk with people."

That's a classic example of how different objectives can ruin a business. Obviously, Dave was focused only on getting to his own engineering objective, which was also obviously at odds with the objective of the production line employees.

Because the Great Divide creates this selfish "fiefdom" mentality, it's the number one problem in corporate America today, and it will remain so tomorrow. As a result, companies have been unable to integrate effectively the crucial strategies they need to succeed, namely, business, manufacturing, quality, and customer service strategies. For example, with specific financial objectives to meet at the end of a quarter, most corporations willingly sacrifice customer service and product quality in order to meet bottom-line targets. So the dollars-and-cents, bottom-line-driven business strategies do not always coincide with the theories and values that companies have set up for customer service. In the long run, these companies are only shooting themselves in the foot. Nor are Misguided Managers able to cope with the problem because they're simply too busy building their own empires. They never integrate with the other Misguided Managers because they're afraid that if they do, they will lose their power in their own section. What's more, most organizational structures only encourage this disjointedness.

Sometimes, probably most of the time, finding out that your favorite emperor is strolling around buck-naked isn't such an easy thing to accept. I confess that the news would have been unbearable if there had not been something good to say about the process as well. Sure, in a lot of ways it was a big bummer; on the other hand, I gradually began to think there might be a way to change this management dilemma. I didn't know how exactly, but more and more it seemed like the answer probably had something to do with Brandt's pick-up team.

Chapter Three

THE CALM BEFORE THE STORM

My big moment, my chance to try a new approach to management, finally came along about two years after my eyes were opened by Brandt and his team. I was 33 years old and I had just been promoted to general manager of the FineFax plant, the first woman ever to occupy that position in the entire history of Comlinks, Inc. The plant, another Comlinks subsidiary, assembled the well-known FineFax facsimile machine and contributed $100 million to the corporation's consolidated annual revenues. Approximately 400 people worked at FineFax producing three different models of the popular machine on three shifts. To a hard-working girl who had spent the past 10 years coming up the corporate ladder, it was a miracle come true.

In fact, on my first day on the new job, I was shamelessly impressed with myself. I sat there in my office for a few minutes just basking in the glow of it all, rocking back in my leather-upholstered, brass-studded executive chair and taking in the impressive features of the office. The large mahogany desk had been rubbed to a high polish and matched the nearby conference table perfectly; there was a thick, light-gray carpet on the floor, and the walls, done in a subtle mauve color, were hung with the usual all-purpose, but basically peaceful, landscape paintings. The whole place said "management" in big letters.

After I returned to my senses, though, I decided I'd better get to work, so I began studying the plant's financial statements to find out how the business had been running over the past three years. As I tracked the numbers, I saw that sales had been growing about 10 percent a year, but that recently the rate of increase had begun to slow down, and it looked as though the product line's market share had dropped a percentage point or two. Expenses had been increasing by 15 percent a year but had been offset somewhat by declines in raw materials prices; however, it now appeared that profit margins had begun to fall back from their highest points; and finally, product quality sputtered occasionally but overall seemed to be holding up.

Normally, I would've been troubled by the numbers I'd just reviewed, but before I arrived at the plant, senior management had told me not to be overly concerned. In fact, Walter Treddle, Comlinks' regional vice president responsible for FineFax and two other plants in the area, had given me a personal briefing.

You will probably recognize Walter Treddle right off because the more I see of business the more I'm convinced that all of us have to suffer with a Treddle at some point in our careers. My Treddle had been with Comlinks for nearly 25 years. He was in his early fifties, favored dark pinstriped suits, and had a pair of enormous wing-tip shoes that looked like they weighed 20 pounds and might conceivably cause him to hydroplane in a heavy rain. Treddle was a conservative company man through and through, dedicated to preserving the corporate policies and methods that had promoted him. He ruled his domain from an office the size of an aircraft hangar and was known to have a temper invariably brought on whenever any of his subordinates strayed too far from the narrow company line he guarded so vigilantly. It was that temper that had earned him the nickname "Treddle the Terrible."

During my meeting with him, though, Treddle was surprisingly calm, even solicitous. He told me that the slowdown in various financial measurements was merely a normal, temporary adjustment to a market that had attracted many new competitors. Of course, I would have to watch my profit margins and product quality carefully, but that was really nothing more than a routine assignment. In general, Treddle said FineFax was an average plant without any major problems. Then, in an odd tone of voice that placed the remark somewhere between a joke and a threat, he said, "Besides, all you have to do is what I tell you and you won't get into trouble." Treddle had a knack for saying dumb stuff like that.

Treddle's briefing notwithstanding, when I left his office I didn't feel especially secure because I had already reviewed the results for myself and reached a few tentative conclusions. Still, I decided to learn more about FineFax before I made up my mind on what the numbers really meant.

Later that morning, I went over to the main conference room for a presentation by my staff who would update me on current conditions in the plant.

FineFax Layers of Command and Control

General Manager
Plant Manager
Production Manager
Shift Managers
Supervisors
Lead Hands
Employees

Operations

General Manager
Functional Managers
Department Managers
Supervisors
Employees

Support Services

Like most other manufacturing companies, FineFax was organized around the traditional corporate structure of functional responsibilities, including operational and support service departments: personnel/human resources, materials, operations, accounting, information systems, quality/customer service, engineering, and maintenance. Each of these areas (by the way, reading "fiefdoms" here wouldn't be a bad idea either) had a specific chain of command. For example, on the operations side of the business there were seven layers of management, beginning with me, as general manager, and followed by a plant manager, a production manager, shift managers, supervisors, lead hands, and finally, the employees out on the production floor. The support services side of the business had a similar arrangement of five management layers consisting of general manager, functional managers, department managers, supervisors, and employees.

One by one, the managers of each of the plant's functional areas got up to give their reports. It turned out to be nothing less than a self-congratulatory chorus of reassurance, building in confidence with each report.

Personnel/human resources sang out first that the plant's yearly performance review system was working well; there had been no employee complaints, and morale was good.

Quality quickly took up the melody. Yes, there had been a slight decrease in product quality recently, but the cause was known and would be corrected by the next quarter. In addition, quality was proud to say that there were no customer service issues currently and that, moreover, the department had not received a customer complaint in the last six months.

The materials department added a few brief grace notes that it was working smoothly and that raw materials prices were still falling.

And the next few bars from the engineering department were equally brief and sweet. Everything was under control, sang their soloist with noticeable self-satisfaction.

Then production offered a particularly joyous refrain. Efficiencies on the production line looked terrific and so did scrap rates. True, overtime had been running a bit high, but it was entirely manageable.

Finally, information systems echoed the prevailing optimism, but then closed with a subdued rendition of their usual lament that they needed more people to clear up a backlog.

It was all music to my ears, a beautiful symphony. I floated back to my office and saw in my mind a future so full of promise that it even included a momentary daydream in which yours truly had become a corporate vice president.

"I guess Treddle was right after all," I thought. "I really don't have much to worry about. Everything sounds great. I've got a great team, and they're all working well together, and there are no major issues here. Life is good."

But even here, when my prospects seemed uniformly bright, some part of me would not let me abandon myself completely to the superficial pleasure of the moment. How could it be, I found myself wondering, that FineFax had somehow been spared the problems I'd seen in so many other plants? Was FineFax truly some kind of rare exception in which the usual differences between managers and employees did not exist?

What had been happening to me, I can tell you now in hindsight, is pretty much every plant's first greeting to an Unmanager-in-the-making. More times than not, the status quo will show a false face as it tries to cover up and resist change.

There's only one remedy. You've got to get out of your office, see the production floor firsthand, and talk with the people who work there.

And that was exactly where I headed next.

Chapter Four

THROUGH THE
LOOKING GLASS

A t lunchtime that first day, I decided to visit with production employees in the plant cafeteria, maybe even share lunch with them. Admittedly, this was not the way I usually conducted myself at work; I usually communicated with employees through my staff, as I had been trained to do. But I was getting better at the fine art of just hanging out and, besides, today was different. I had been so pumped up by my staff's briefing that I felt I could allow myself to be, well, unconventional. Anyway, as I saw it, what could be the harm in such a visit? Hadn't I been told the plant was running smoothly, that employees had no complaints? Clearly we would all be lunching together as members of what was basically a big mutual admiration society.

So I set out for the cafeteria in high spirits. However, I had barely left the management office area when a small, but persistent, inner voice suddenly began to warn me that I had made a big mistake. And the voice only grew louder the farther I walked.

It was dingy out there in production. Dirty, dark, industrial green paint was peeling in spots from the walls; papers and crushed boxes were lying around on the floor, which itself appeared to be smudged with some kind of oil stain.

When I reached the cafeteria, I got in line and ordered soup and a sandwich. At the same time I noticed uneasily that most of the employees seemed to have brought their own lunch. I wondered if they knew something I didn't know. Then I asked Frasier McNeal, Bob Westwood, and Mary Sue Dalton, who were already seated at one of the nearby tables, if I could join them. I introduced myself as the new general manager. The three employees gave me a so-so welcome that was cordial enough, but you sure couldn't say they were wildly enthusiastic.

I took a taste of my soup, which was cold, not hot as advertised, and then asked with the kind of bluff, good humor meant to show that I was just another player on the same team, "Well, hey, how're things going here anyway?"

There was a pause as the employees looked at each other. Nobody said a word for several minutes, so I decided to change the subject. We could come back to it later.

"So, I notice most of you brought your own lunches. Is that a comment on the cafeteria food?"

Mary Sue chuckled a little and said, "Well, I guess you could say so. It's somewhat inconsistent, and most of us have learned not to take our chances."

"Inconsistent?" I was puzzled. "Hasn't anyone complained about this to a manager?"

The three of them glanced at each other then looked down. I was finally starting to catch on.

"Look," I said, "I really want to know the truth. I want to take your comments seriously. Please be honest. You can trust me."

Perhaps it was my tone of voice, or maybe it was because I was new, or maybe it was because my good reputation had preceded me, but after a little more silence, Mary Sue finally asked "Do you really want to know?" And with that, my inner voice scolded me, "Trisha, my girl. Big mistake. Big."

During the next 20 minutes, I heard a description of life in the plant from the employees' point of view that made me wonder if my staff had actually been talking about some other company. The employees said they hadn't spoken to a general manager in maybe three years nor had they seen much of any other manager. When I named a few managers on my staff, they seemed only vaguely aware of who they were.

But not seeing management was far from their only concern, and they went on to list several more problems. The performance review system was screwed up, they said, because supervisors played favorites and their "golden child" of the moment always got the best review rather than the person doing the best job. They said the employee often did not have the right tools or training to do their jobs; the production schedule changed five times a day, and they never knew what they would be working on next; the machines broke down frequently; and they had no clear idea whether the job they were doing was good or bad.

When I asked about quality, the employees said that they simply didn't know if they had a quality problem or not and that I would have to take that question up with the quality inspectors. And, no, again, they were never told how the business was doing in general. Finally, I asked them what the human resources department's response had been when they learned about these problems. The employees told me that, in fact, no one would ever go to human resources because human resources would rat to management; then the person who came in with the information invariably was written up for one thing or another in the weeks ahead. Which, for me, was also a pretty good explanation of why every so often the employees looked around nervously as they talked.

When the employees left to return to the production line, I had to stay behind for a while to compose myself. "This is incredible," I thought. "I just took this job. I thought this was going to be a piece of cake. What the hell is going on? Why am I getting these different stories?"

After lunch I took a tour of the plant with the plant manager, and the news didn't get any better. The production line had definite problems. Work on the line itself proceeded in a strictly linear flow: raw materials came in, the circuit boards were put together, the boards were tested to make sure the parts were connecting properly, then the boards were combined with the fax housing and other hardware, and finally the whole unit was given a functional test. In theory, this production process was simple enough, but in practice the course of events became more tortured. Between each step in the assembly line, the work in process had to be placed in storage areas to make sure that the circuit boards and hardware would arrive at the same place at the same time and in sufficient quantity. Thus, rather than assembling, testing, and shipping, the assembly line actually assembled, inspected, repaired, stored, tested, repaired, inspected, stored, assembled, conducted final tests, stored, and then shipped. Plus, the storage areas — as if to highlight their bad influence on the process — were surrounded by wire cages.

I also noticed that although some employees were working industriously, others were idle because their test equipment had broken down. And right then a loud horn sounded, and everybody on the line marched off for a break like the employee robots I'd been thinking about.

It was a Maalox moment. Worse still, the pain seemed to sharpen as the tour progressed. For example, when I walked into the engineering department, I thought it curious that the place was packed with engineers even though there appeared to be more than enough work for them out on the production floor. Similarly, the atmosphere in the accounting department also seemed out of whack — excessively clinical and secretive with folder after folder marked "classified" or "confidential." And the quality department seemed to have a life of its own, cut off from the rest of the plant where the inspectors and the staff were exercising their calculators furiously and making up bar charts. I found no peace of mind in the inventory stockroom either. Although the inventory was neatly arranged, suggesting that there was some sort of system at work within the materials group, there was an awful lot of inventory; I mean it was everywhere. In fact, between raw materials and finished goods, the stockroom was actually larger than the production area. Nor was human resources any more satisfying. The department was fully staffed, but there wasn't an employee in sight. A large pile of company newsletters stood in a corner of the room, and near the door there was a suggestion box locked with a big padlock. The inscription on the box said, "We keep your suggestions confidential."

It's simply amazing what you can learn when you start wandering around a plant. For example, in contrast to the happy face worn by the department manager, an engineer happened to tell me that his department didn't have a budget big enough to do all that was being asked of it; the test equipment was frequently out of service because they had not received enough of the specialized training necessary to maintain it effectively; and furthermore, they could not get maintenance to store the correct spare parts. And a guy in the materials department was equally direct, saying they were really gasping for breath because orders kept changing all the time; they could never get the right amount of product in finished goods, so they simply had to build more of everything than they needed. But their biggest issue centered on the information systems department which, for some unknown reason, couldn't get them the reports they needed to track demand on time and prepare better schedules.

For the most part I was able to maintain my composure even though the news was often disturbing. There were times when the facts nearly knocked me off my feet. For example, here's a little story about how I learned the truth about the plant's quality control measurements.

A Question of Quality

I had a conversation with Franklin Dell, one of the plant's senior quality inspectors. Now Franklin is your typical button-down, no frills, meticulously groomed, quality person. Every hair is in place; his tie matches his jacket, which matches his socks, which match his shoes. Not that there's anything wrong with this, mind you. He looks like a man of standards, as one would expect of someone in his position. He also looks like a man who knows the importance of toeing the line. Someone, perhaps, Walter Treddle would approve of.

At any rate, I asked him to explain the plant's quality standard for me.

"For which customer?" Franklin asked.

"Pardon me," I said, "but what do you mean 'which customer'?"

"Well," he said, "some won't mind if the telephone buttons are a little loose, but others will just go nuts. Then, too, it depends on whether the customer is in another plant within the company or is a domestic or foreign customer."

"Wait a minute, Franklin," I said. "Let me get this straight. Are you telling me that there are different standards for different customers?"

"Exactly," Franklin said.

"But shouldn't there be only one standard?"

"Certainly would make my job a lot easier," Franklin said, "but when I suggested as much some time ago, no one seemed very interested."

I thanked him and staggered off.

I nearly died when I discovered that FineFax not only lacked a single, consistent quality standard but that FineFax also seemed quite content to modify whatever standards there were to make itself look good. And not much later, I discovered that a similar situation existed in customer service. After a few rough calculations, I found that if there had been only one standard for all customers, the number of quality defects reported would have increased significantly. I also found that if the method of measuring customer service had likewise been applied consistently, complaints would not be zero as claimed, but in fact would be well above average and rising.

Overall, it would be safe to say that the day had not lived up to its early promise. The face FineFax had shown me at the start had indeed been false. Although I couldn't yet clearly identify all the underlying problems, the experience bothered me so much that the next morning I called my staff together to discuss some of my observations.

It was a strange meeting from the start because the managers of the various functional departments were much more interested in discrediting the employees I had talked with at lunch than they were in listening to my comments. Naturally, news of that lunch meeting had traveled the production floor grapevine rapidly, and the participants were known to practically everybody by quitting time. The managers had had time to prepare themselves and now spent some time trying to deflect my criticisms by joking about the meeting, while at the same time sandbagging the individuals involved.

One manager said, "Well, Trisha, that was some lunch you had the other day. Man, those people went right off the chart on you." All the other managers laughed as their way of confirming the fantastic truth of their colleague's statement.

"What do you mean by that, John?" I asked.

"Of course, you couldn't know these things because you're new," John said, "but you remember that girl, Mary Sue? Well, she's a troublemaker from way back. You can't really listen to her, and she's always agitating for a union in here." The other managers now murmured together gravely, frequently repeating words like *trouble, union,* and *agitate.*

"And don't forget about Bob," another manager announced. "He does good work, but he gets way too excited, I mean, like hysterical. He can be a major mental case at times." The managers shook their heads in exaggerated sympathy over Bob's problems.

I parried by launching into my observations, but the managers continued their strategy of deflection.

"I'm concerned about inventory," I said.

"Why?" a manager asked. "You should have seen it three years ago."

"I'm concerned that the employees don't know about quality defects," I said.

"Well, right," a manager said. "We don't want to get them distracted from building the product. When they're building it wrong, we sure let them know. You can count on that."

In general, each manager's response translated into something like: "I'm in charge of my territory, and I know what I'm doing, and everything is fine."

By now it was fairly clear that FineFax had not escaped the typical schizophrenic breakdown between managers and employees. In fact, the Great Divide between the two was so wide you could fly a plane through it. But I decided not to make an issue of it quite yet. What I did do, though, was tell these managers that during the next two weeks before our next scheduled meeting, I would be very pleased if they could reduce the inventory storage areas, fix the test equipment problem on the production line, and get the plant cleaned up. I also said that, judging from what I had heard at lunch, morale was low, and I would like to know why.

"I don't want to have another lunch like that again," I said in closing. I heard a slight grunt from over in the corner. It was Dave Ballard, the plant's production manager. Dave, who had been with the company a long time, was known as someone who spouted company policy. He reminded me of myself when I naively thought I should follow "command-and-control" leadership so that I would be considered an effective manager. I also sensed that he was someone not used to seeing women in management positions, although this was more of an intuition on my part, rather than the result of any specific action I'd seen. In spite of that, he probably would make a good politician in another lifetime. He knew how to "play the game."

So when I mentioned that I didn't want to hear any more negative comments from employees, Dave said, "Don't worry, Trisha, you won't. We'll make sure no one ever tells you stuff like that again." He said it a little ominously, which made me uneasy. I wish I knew what he had in mind so I could have stopped it.

Chapter Five

MAJOR

DISAPPOINTMENTS

I guess it must have been a few days before my next scheduled meeting with my staff when I went for a stroll through the plant to see how things were going. At first, I was encouraged by what I saw — the plant had been cleaned up a bit, the paper and crushed boxes were gone from the floors, and the peeling paint was patched up. Unfortunately, the longer I stayed out there I could tell that beyond these few cosmetic touch-ups, none of the other changes I had asked for had been made. The production lines looked exactly as they did on my first day; inventory was still everywhere; the test equipment was still down; and elsewhere, the engineers were still packed in their offices, and the human resources people were still busy at work talking to themselves.

But all these disappointments were only moderately unpleasant compared to the pain of the startling brush-off I got from Mary Sue Dalton, one of the employees in the original lunch party. I had spotted her walking along one of the production lines, and I called out to her hoping to visit for a few minutes. But instead of waiting for me to catch up, Mary Sue, with the other employees looking on, turned away and headed off in another direction. I was upset and embarrassed. I took off after her and when I finally overtook her, I asked to see her in my office in five minutes.

"So what's the problem?" I asked when she arrived. "You know, I really don't appreciate being treated like that."

"Well, I just didn't see you, that's all," she said.

"C'mon," I said, "I know you saw me. So what's up?"

"Look," she said, "I apologize for doing that to you. You didn't deserve it. It wasn't your problem. It's just that I've about had it with the supervisors."

"What do you mean?" I asked. "What about the supervisors? What's going on with them?"

"Oh, nothing at all," she said, "except that they've already given me enough bad performance write-ups in the last two weeks to kill a dog. I mean, I was written up for being a troublemaker and having a bad attitude, and another time for talking to you without going through the chain of command or something like that. It's all crap. And I've been told that I've been a troublemaker for years even though I've gotten the highest productivity ratings you can get. And frankly, I knew I shouldn't have talked to management anyway, so from now on I'll just keep my mouth shut and do my job."

I was stunned by what I had just heard and almost sick that a mere lunchroom conversation could ever have produced such a disastrous fallout. At the same time, I recalled the managers promising me that they would make sure the employees never talked to me that way again and realized that they had intended something entirely different from what I had thought.

I wasn't in a good mood at the staff meeting a few days later, and I asked the managers why so little had been done on the improvements I had asked for. There were many excuses. The people in production went on about how they really didn't have any time because they had to turn out product, and besides a quality issue came up and they all had to focus on that. And the folks from human resources offered a report that attempted to document that the people I had spoken with were basically all complainers and agitators of one stripe or another.

When I couldn't stand it any longer, I told them how I had been embarrassed publicly by an employee. Then I asked if any of the other people I had eaten lunch with had been written up. And why wasn't I surprised to learn that they all had?

At that point, I lost my temper. I told them that unless there were some really strong arguments against it, I wanted all the write-ups removed from the files. I went on to say that I wanted any employee to be able to talk to me at any time and that if I heard one more time of employees being written up for expressing their opinions, well, I would just think of a way for human resources to die a thousand deaths.

Finally, I said solemnly that it was crystal clear to me now that the FineFax plant had to mend its ways and that we'd all be starting a big campaign to do just that.

Everybody was looking at each other, and you could almost hear the "dum-dee-dum-dum" theme music from *Dragnet* kick in. Maybe it was a bit too dramatic, but what the hell, sometimes you've got to get people's attention. Besides, it wasn't drama I was worrying about — I had another problem on my mind.

Chapter Six

SIR ISAAC TRISHA

When I got home that day after meeting with my staff over that write-up mess, I was in bad shape. At first I was just extremely frustrated with the staff, but after a while another feeling began to creep in on me. I was scared.

I realized I had just made a big deal out of telling my staff that FineFax had to mend its ways and then, on top of that, I had announced that we were all going to start a big improvement campaign. Unfortunately, the problem with all this was that I really didn't know what to do next. Yes, I knew we needed to break down barriers between managers and employees and change employee training, but I didn't have a concrete plan. I could tell you what the problems were in most corporations, but I wasn't so sure about solutions. At the same time, I was trying to find some organizing principle that would capture my ideas and package all my notions and thoughts together so I could easily tell other people about them. And if that wasn't enough, I was also very concerned about my ability to do the job. I kept asking myself, "How are you going to manage this stuff? You're already managing as fast as you can; how are you going to manage more?" What I needed was an inspiration, some bolt from the sky — and I needed it soon.

As I recall, it was later that evening, I guess around 8 p.m. when it struck me. I had just put my two kids to bed, and I was sitting in the TV room with my husband Harrison. There was a special report about how managers throughout corporate America were reevaluating their approaches to running their businesses. The old ways simply weren't working anymore. The domestic economy was slowing down at the same time that foreign competition was picking up, and there were grave concerns about the country's economic future. Every industry seemed to have the same solution for the problem, popularly known as the "Do More with Less" solution. Under this plan, businesses were closing plants and offices and laying off employees, an activity they were calling "downsizing" or "reengineering." And then when the managers had lopped off enough heads, they were supposed to manage what was left more intensely.

It was all too true. It was also depressing, and after a while I stopped watching in favor of reading an article in a back issue of *Business Week*. The article described a study into the causes of a number of fatal airplane crashes and close calls; it concluded that the primary reason was a lack of communication and teamwork between captain and crew. In short, lives were actually being lost because of poor management in the cockpit.

The study had found that often the captain of the plane was so dictatorial and intimidating that the other members of the crew simply would not speak up, even when they knew there was a problem at hand. In one example, a co-pilot had warned the captain that they were exceeding the required speed only to be told, "I'll do what I want . . . just look out the damn windows."

That article blew my mind. Here was a particularly vivid example of just how disastrous the Great Divide, the gap between managers and employees, could be. How many times during my own career had I seen senior managers treat other employees just like the captain in the cockpit had treated his crew? Worse still, I myself had been guilty of the very same dictatorial, "do-what-I-say," "listen-to-no-one-else," management style. Granted, the results weren't as graphic, but the Great Divide management approach was certainly causing companies to go down in flames. And it was all because perfectly capable people weren't being allowed to do their jobs to the best of their abilities.

That's when it all came together for me, like Newton bopped on the head by that falling apple. I remembered how, at my old job, without any intervention by management, Brandt and his pick-up team had once organized themselves so effectively to meet a crisis.

"Unmanagement," I yelled.

My husband, who was tuning in the HBO channel, jumped at the sudden outburst and joked, "No, I don't think so, Trisha. I think they're showing *Mission Impossible* tonight."

But I barely heard him because I was busy scribbling down my breakthrough in the margin of the magazine so I wouldn't forget it.

The Unmanager's Creed

The point is not so much doing more with less, but rather deciding who should be doing what — and then letting them do it. The point is not to manage more but to manage less.

There it was — the answer to my fears. I mean, think of what I had just realized. I didn't have to take the whole world on my shoulders and try to manage this change in management all by myself. That wasn't it at all. The point was that I had to let the employees manage themselves; I had to get them involved in actually running the business. It was all summed up in my new organizing principle — Unmanagement. "Doing More with Less" wasn't the cure for what was ailing corporate America at all. In fact, if you left Unmanagement out of the picture, it was entirely likely that the "downsize/manage more" approach would produce a company just as screwed up, but smaller.

Maybe I still didn't exactly have what you'd call a "concrete plan," but I was certainly a lot more focused than I had ever been. Now I felt that I could at least make a presentation. And so what if I didn't know all the answers. Now, with Unmanagement, I was supposed to let people in the plant help me figure out the rest of it.

Chapter Seven

WE'RE NOT IN
KANSAS ANYMORE

T hat lightning bolt of inspiration had me all wound up. I had been scribbling away furiously and by the time I got back to the plant on Monday, I had already come up with six of what would later become the Ten Principles of Unmanagement. I wasn't all that clear on the exact order of many of them, and I suspected that many of them would be going on more or less simultaneously. But I did know that "Identify and Accept the Need to Change" had to come first.

To begin a program of Unmanagement, a manager must demonstrate conclusively that it's imperative that his or her place of business change its way of doing business. Changing the status quo under most circumstances is extremely difficult, but without a very compelling reason to change with which people can identify, it's nearly impossible. It's important to raise a convincing banner that will rally people to the cause. At the same time, we had to keep in mind the following guidelines.

How to Get Change Started

- The leader of the business unit involved (the general manager in my case) should initiate change to signal its importance and establish its legitimacy. Although it is true that the standard-bearer may emerge from any management level, eventually commitment to change must reach to the highest executive levels if Unmanagement is to realize its maximum potential.

  The need to change is almost always made up of two parts: external demands related to prevailing market conditions and internal process and organization issues within the business itself. The leader can be particularly helpful in describing the external market conditions that demand change. In fact, given how tightly information is controlled within corporations, the leader will usually be the only person in the company with enough facts to address the subject at all.

- The leader must never command or dictate change. The leader can only facilitate change. Change without ownership will always fail in the long run.

- Employees must always be involved from the very beginning. You must have their voluntary and ongoing commitment. What's more, this is the only way they will experience "ownership" in the Unmanagement process.

- The stronger the need, the stronger the desire to fill it. Business survival is always a hard need to beat.

With all this rattling around in my brain, I holed up in my office for a couple days to outline my presentation and work up a few flip charts. Then I had to figure out how to give my talk. It proved to be a little more difficult than it looked. The objective was to involve the entire plant, but I didn't want to stop the work flow completely to do it, and I didn't want to ask people for their free time if I could help it. So what we did was break up the entire workforce on all three shifts into groups of 20 to 30 people, and we rotated through the entire plant. Using the cafeteria as our central meeting room, I'd talk to one group of 20 people, or two groups of 40 when I could; then they'd go back to the production floor to relieve the next group of 20 so I could talk to them. It took me the better part of a week to get to everybody, and I had to appear on each of the shifts, which didn't help my home life much. But believe me, it is the best way to do it. You get to meet everybody up close and personal, and you can use this technique again and again because there will be many other times when you'll want to reach the entire plant with something more than a memo on a bulletin board.

Once I got my scheduling worked out, I was ready to step up to the podium. Basically, in my presentation I outlined what external factors were forcing a change; then I linked those external events to internal problems in the plant. Then I described as best I could, the new direction I was taking and how that would affect the way things were done; and finally, I asked for help — lots of help.

Here's what I had to say. One of the managers taped one of my talks and gave it to me later. I had it typed up because I thought you might like to look it over to get a few ideas for yourself. Feel free to use as much of it as you like. I didn't alter the transcript much, except that I inserted copies of my charts. Somebody started calling it the "We're Not in Kansas Anymore" speech, and the name stuck.

The "We're Not in Kansas Anymore" Speech

The business world isn't what it used to be.

If FineFax — or any other company for that matter — expects to survive, we're going to have to adapt to the new world out there; we're going to have to make some serious changes in the way we do things. It's definitely "crunch time" for us all.

Some of those changes are "external," which means they're brought on by external conditions in the marketplace outside the company, and other changes will be "internal" because they're called for by conditions inside our company.

Let me start with the external changes first.

For a long time — throughout the 1960s, 1970s, and even into the 1980s — business was able to approach the customer with the attitude: "I am king. This is the product I make and you, customer, you don't have any choice but to buy it as is." But that attitude won't cut it anymore; competition is simply too intense. Now business has to have a new attitude: "I am the one who has to serve the customer." Businesses have to become very involved with their customers to find out what they want. Customers are king now, and they're not at all shy when business does not provide what they want.

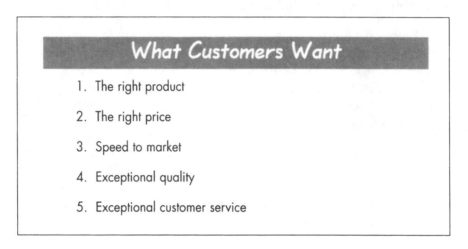

What Customers Want

1. The right product

2. The right price

3. Speed to market

4. Exceptional quality

5. Exceptional customer service

And needless to say, the customer will only become more demanding in the years ahead.

We have to ask ourselves immediately, "Are we meeting those customer demands here at FineFax today?" Naturally, we'd all like to think that we are, but there's another way of finding out that doesn't rely so heavily on wishful thinking: we look at our actual business results and then we compare those results against a major competitor. Take a look for yourself.

Our sales are rising, but recently their rate of increase has begun to slow down. It also appears that we're losing small percentages of our market share. Finally, our profit margins, while still relatively high, are beginning to lose ground bit by bit. Now some corporate managers like to say that, given the many new companies entering the fax market, FineFax's results really aren't all that bad, that all the results really say is that we're a company adjusting naturally and reasonably well to a much more crowded marketplace. Unfortunately, after comparing our figures against those of FaxQuick, Inc., our leading competitor, it isn't so easy to swallow the corporate point of view. FaxQuick doesn't seem to know that the market is more crowded.

FineFax:	FaxQuick:
Sales: ↑ 10%	↑ 19%
Market Share: ↓ 2%	↑ 7%
Expenses: ↑ 15%	No Information
Raw Materials Prices: ↓ 5%	↓ 5% Assumption
Profit Margin: ↓ 5%	No Information
Quality Defects: ↓ 3%	No Information

Their sales are still rising at a good clip, and they even seem to have gained market share. At the same time, their margins are improving.

I'm afraid there's only one conclusion to be drawn from this comparison. Although I'm sure we'd all like to believe otherwise, it certainly looks as though FineFax is not meeting the customer needs that we listed above as well as its competition. Customers want to buy from FaxQuick more than they do from us.

And that means we have to look inward. We've identified the needs for change coming from the external marketplace, and we have found that we are not currently addressing those needs satisfactorily. Now we must find out why, which means in turn that we must identify the needs for change coming from within our own company.

You've all seen me wandering around the plant over the past several weeks. Well, I've talked to a lot of people, and because you've all been so helpful, I've been able to spot a number of problems that I think are harming our business. These problems fall into five distinct areas:

Let me explain what I mean.

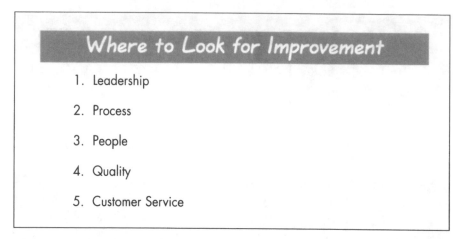

Where to Look for Improvement

1. Leadership

2. Process

3. People

4. Quality

5. Customer Service

Our leadership is ineffective. There's a big gap between managers and employees at FineFax, and the two are not communicating very well at all. Many of our processes, such as the cages on the production lines, are too cumbersome and slow. Our people don't feel a sense of ownership in our business, and they seem very frustrated. And finally, we do not have uniform standards for either quality control or customer service, and there is reason to believe that, contrary to what we may think, we are not excelling in either area. If we let this situation continue, FineFax surely will not survive for long.

Your first reaction will probably be, "Hell, we'll just manage our way out of the problem. We'll manage harder; we'll manage more."

I have to ask you, though, do you seriously think you could do that? From what I've seen, you've already got about as much as you can handle, and the level of job stress around here is already high enough.

But if we can't manage more, then what can we do?

I know it may sound crazy, but I really believe that the answer is to manage less. Or to put it another way: we can "Unmanage."

Okay, okay, calm down. I said I knew it sounded crazy. Just hear me out.

When you look at that list of what customers will be demanding of business in the future, one conclusion should stand out — those demands are so broad and so complex that no one segment of a company could possibly get the job done, particularly given the intense competition in world markets today. No, management certainly can't do it alone; instead, everyone must be involved.

I said earlier that business isn't what it used to be, and I really believe that business has entered a new era that will require an unprecedented amount of trust, cooperation, and interaction between management and employee. That's why I think the future will require Unmanagement. And what is Unmanagement? Here's what it means to me.

Unmanagement Defined

Unmanagement is an approach to running a business in which employees direct their own work because many of the responsibilities traditionally restricted to management have been shared with the entire employee population.

And what do you have to do to practice Unmanagement? Frankly, I'm not really sure because I don't know that it's ever been done before, and I suspect that we'll all be learning the answer together. But I have given it a lot of thought and I've come up with six ideas or principles that we can start out with.

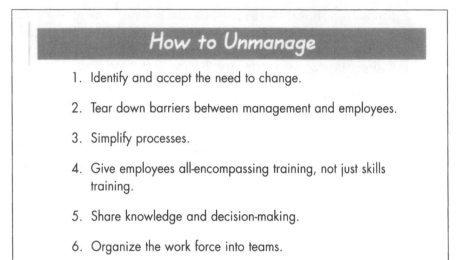

How to Unmanage

1. Identify and accept the need to change.

2. Tear down barriers between management and employees.

3. Simplify processes.

4. Give employees all-encompassing training, not just skills training.

5. Share knowledge and decision-making.

6. Organize the work force into teams.

Overall, I want to say that I think Unmanagement is the one method that will enable us to coordinate our business, production, and customer service strategies so we can give customers what they want. It will eliminate the gap between managers and employees that has existed for too long and the fiefdom mentality that currently rules daily life at FineFax. Most companies will give way to a new arrangement.

Here, in this diagram, you can see what I mean by "new arrangement":

Direct Labor has been toned, honed, and trained to be the company's first line of defense. That means they've been trained and empowered to act immediately on their own whenever they spot a problem rather than wait around for management to happen by. And the Supervisor has become a "Facilitator" who coaches, counsels, and trains people to act independently. The Leadership team, or senior management, actively supports what's going on. They're doing crisis intervention — only coming in when they need to. But they're monitoring the total process continually and creating an environment in which it can thrive. Materials is now working closely with the people in production to schedule priorities; they're reducing work in process between departments; and they've started doing their forecasting

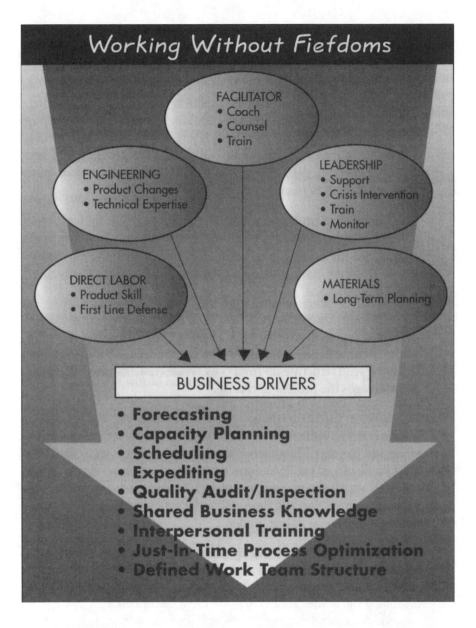

Working Without Fiefdoms

FACILITATOR
- Coach
- Counsel
- Train

ENGINEERING
- Product Changes
- Technical Expertise

LEADERSHIP
- Support
- Crisis Intervention
- Train
- Monitor

DIRECT LABOR
- Product Skill
- First Line Defense

MATERIALS
- Long-Term Planning

BUSINESS DRIVERS

- **Forecasting**
- **Capacity Planning**
- **Scheduling**
- **Expediting**
- **Quality Audit/Inspection**
- **Shared Business Knowledge**
- **Interpersonal Training**
- **Just-In-Time Process Optimization**
- **Defined Work Team Structure**

based on current demand rather than historical patterns. Engineering is now asking people if they understand the various operating procedures rather than issuing instructions and then walking away as they did in the past.

Each group still carries on with those skills unique to the group. But the major difference here is that the groups are also, at the same time, involved in all the other tasks essential to running a business — tasks that were previously outside their responsibility and formal job description. Things like capacity planning, scheduling, expediting, and quality inspection are no longer the single focus of any one group or individual — they are everybody's job. For example, engineering will still do the capacity planning, but now the materials group and the employees will get a chance to sign off on the plans before those plans are sent on to management and put in place.

Now you're probably saying to yourselves, "Oh my God, she's going to reorganize and restructure the whole place. No more engineering, no more quality, no more this, no more that." But you're wrong. We're not reorganizing; we are redefining roles. Here's how I see it.

The organizational structure of a company will take care of itself once the company starts sharing knowledge, objectives, and responsibilities. Structure is an outcome of the process, not the beginning step. Tinkering with structure up front only creates useless wheel-spinning and sabotages the process of change.

I want us all to think of ourselves, starting right now, as Unmanagement pioneers because we really will be setting out on an adventure together. There is no handy map to guide us, at least not that I know of, and we'll just have to improvise as we go along. I think our best plan is to improve leadership, process, people, quality, and customer service, one at a time, using the six Unmanagement principles we've got so far as our guides.

And, please, if you come up with any more principles along the way, let's add them to our list and give them a try.

I thought the whole thing had gone great, and I had already received a lot of good feedback from people as well. But wouldn't you know there had to be something to bring me down. After my last meeting, I had to drive the five miles over to Comlinks' regional headquarters building to attend a management seminar on plant safety. I was still exhilarated from my Unmanagement presentation, and I had trouble concentrating at the seminar, but I kept reminding myself not to get too carried away. There was an enormous amount of work ahead and, besides, reality had a way of bursting even the brightest bubbles. It turned out to be good advice and exactly at the right moment. As I was leaving the seminar, Walter Treddle, the regional vice president who worked in the same building, stopped me in the hallway and asked me to come into his office and talk with him for a while. Right away I got a headache. I had no idea what he had on his mind, but I knew he had not been given his nickname, "Treddle the Terrible," for his small talk.

"I hear you had a big meeting over at the plant," Treddle said. "How did it turn out?"

"It was fantastic," I said. "Couldn't have gone better."

"Let's see, what was it," Treddle said, "something like . . . ah, yes . . . 'nonmanagement,' that's it, isn't it?"

"No, Walter," I said. "It's actually Unmanagement. There's a big difference."

"Oh, of course," Treddle said. "How silly of me."

"Maybe it would help if I told you a little about it," I said.

"No, I don't think so," Treddle said. "I've already heard a lot, and I want to tell you that I don't like what I'm hearing, not at all."

And now, all pretense cast aside, Treddle began a lengthy and extraordinary monologue. Among other things, he told me that employees were not prepared for independence, that history had demonstrated conclusively that giving employees too much independence only confused them and made them unhappy. In fact, he said, employees even preferred being given orders every day because when they went home, they did not have to think about their jobs anymore.

"It's really pretty simple," Treddle said in conclusion. "Unmanagement is, well, unnatural. I'm sure you'll agree in light of everything I've talked about."

"Well, Walter," I said, "it's definitely something for me to think about." And I got up to leave.

"Not so fast, Trish. I don't like seeing people change things around here. But since you're new, I'll make a deal with you. I'll give you 60 days. If I don't see any considerable improvements that help us meet our business objectives, I'm afraid I'll have to find a project more suitable to your talents."

And with that challenge ringing in my ears, I left. My drive back to FineFax seemed endless. I went over my meeting with Treddle again and again. It was very difficult for me to develop a single point of view. On the one hand, I found his opinions outrageous; but on the other, I had to admit that it wasn't too long ago when even I half-believed such nonsense. Donald Brandt's pick-up team had changed my life; obviously Treddle had yet to see the light.

And there was something else that troubled me. Even granting that Comlinks' grapevine was world-class, Treddle still seemed to have more information about the Unmanagement meeting than any grapevine could provide. I tried to fight off the thought, but it kept coming back. "Could somebody be reporting to Treddle?" I wondered. "Could there be a mole on my staff?"

Chapter Eight

GREAT EXPECTATIONS

When I was putting my "Kansas" speech together, I struggled unsuccessfully with an idea that I thought would be important to the success of Unmanagement, and I still felt that way after the speech was over. You see, I saw FineFax as kind of a dysfunctional family in search of a new identity, and I'd wanted to find a way to describe what that identity was. One of the first solutions that came to mind was to write up a "vision" statement. But I just couldn't get anywhere with the thought; I couldn't seem to make myself believe in vision statements. I guess I had seen too many of them that were nothing more than wishful thinking. Vision statements never seemed to go far enough. And they never seemed connected to practical, everyday business results. I couldn't deal with it, so I set the idea aside.

Given all those reservations, you can imagine how surprised I was to find that I had come to believe in vision statements — converted from my former sinful ways — only a few days after my speech. For me, the secret lay in discovering that a good vision statement was never meant to stand alone. Instead, it was one of three integrated pieces, which together express the company's vision, along with business objectives and core values. That little revelation came out in a remarkable series of three brainstorming sessions. The purpose of these gatherings was to let a representative group of four managers and supervisors and four employees critique my speech.

And from there we intended to go on to figure out how we could actually implement the Unmanagement principles I had tentatively identified in my speech.

Things did not go as planned. Here are a few excerpts from the diary I was keeping.

Brainstorming Session One:

Stuart Has a Vision

We had barely sat down in the small conference room near my office when Stuart Fallon, a circuit board assembly person on the first shift, announced that before anything else could be done, FineFax absolutely needed a new "vision" to guide its future. He said he'd just read in a major business magazine that this "vision" could produce all kinds of wonders such as focusing the business, inspiring a sense of ownership in the business, and creating a framework for problem solving.

Stuart may not have been an MBA, but he was very persuasive. Pretty soon he had everybody in that room agreeing that a vision statement was essential. They were far less certain, however, about the specific content of that vision. And that fact inspired a vigorous exchange of views, including the comment two employees made that "independent decision making" should be part of the vision. The group kept to its work, and just before members adjourned for the day, they did manage to come up with a concise statement of the new FineFax vision, to wit:

The FineFax Vision

We strive to be an innovative leader in the telecommunications industry by simplifying our processes, reducing our costs, and increasing productivity with constantly improving quality and customer service and by creating an environment in which employees can actively participate in running the business.

I liked the words well enough. I mean, what's to hate? But it still wasn't enough to get a nonbeliever like I was to see the light. I needed more convincing, and as it turned out, more was on the way.

Brainstorming Session Two:

Developing the Right Tactics

At the second brainstorming session, the group members came up with what I thought was a wonderful insight that really got my attention. In the process of writing the vision, they decided that although the vision was an excellent way to guide the overall aspirations of the company, daily production demands required much more specific targets. The vision was the basic statement of strategy, and now they needed some tactics, some concrete business objectives.

It was a memorable moment. For one thing, connecting vision to business objectives was a significant breakthrough in itself. And for another, the group had taken on a particularly tough job. Although we didn't fully appreciate it at the time, defining objectives is always one of the most difficult tasks new Unmanagers have to undertake because usually they're still under the spell of the old fiefdom mentality. In fact, when the subject was first introduced, our group — which we now had to broaden to include more departments — came up with nearly 100 different and competing objectives. For example, the materials people saw objectives from their own particular point of view, and their conclusions were invariably at odds with engineering. The one thing everybody was able to agree on was that every objective, no matter what it was, had to be quantifiable and measurable. It simply wasn't good enough to say you wanted customer service to improve — you also had to say by how much. Eventually, after terrific wrangling and consternation, everyone agreed on five objectives.

The FineFax Objectives

1. Reduce operating costs by 20%.

2. Reduce finished goods inventory by 30%.

3. Improve manufacturing cycle time by 30% from order input to order delivery.

4. Reduce the number of reported quality defects by 35% year to year.

5. Reduce the total number of customer complaints by 35% year to year.

Linking the vision statement to business results answered one of my major problems with the whole idea of vision statements. What's more, the completion of the objectives list was also a milestone in the history of FineFax. For the first time the new Unmanagers had grasped the idea that there could be life beyond fiefdoms and that it was possible to work together toward common objectives. The objectives list also brought to light an Unmanagement rule worth remembering:

The Numbers Have to Be Good

Unmanagement is not a metaphysical diversion. The success of Unmanagement must always be measured in hard business results. Unmanagement is good for the soul, but it also must be good for business.

As I was walking around, out of the corner of my eye, I caught Franklin Dell, the senior quality inspector, writing feverishly on the back of a piece of paper. It seemed to me he was taking very careful notes. I remembered how much information Treddle had learned about Unmanagement. I looked at Franklin again and wondered if he could be the leak.

What I know about Franklin: He'd started at the plant almost 20 years ago in engineering and then moved up through the ranks to his present position as senior quality inspector. He and Treddle were hired around the same time, and while I didn't know for sure, I would guess that the two enjoyed a friendly "good ol' boy" acquaintance. I also seemed to recall that he was the father of two high-school-aged girls. He acts like he respects me, but I wondered if maybe he resents my trying to change things around here? Or maybe he wants my job?

But back to the meeting. I think it was Martha Reynolds from the quality department who first asked me what I thought about quality.

When she first asked me, I had drifted and had to have her repeat the question. I guess I looked at the group with such a blank, wide-eyed stare that several people snickered.

She said, "We were talking about the importance of quality. Since both the vision statement and the business objectives talk about FineFax in terms of 'quantity' and 'what' the company should do, shouldn't something also be said about the 'how' or 'quality' of what the company does?"

In other words, she was asking me if we should acknowledge that the quality of a person's work is just as important as the quantity. I still get goose bumps when I think of it. These people were turning into Unmanagers right before my eyes.

In the prehistoric world of the traditional corporation, it's commonplace for ambitious managers and employees to pursue their objectives at any cost, even if they have to ruthlessly climb over friend and foe alike to get there and leave a trail of bodies in their wake. At heart, the group didn't want to do that anymore, and we were trying to find a way to change. We would resolve that at the next session.

Brainstorming Session Three:
Defining Our Core Values

Eventually, we decided that there was indeed a set of core values that informed both our vision statement and business objectives with the sense of quality we were looking for. We decided to call them the "FineFax Core Values." Someone suggested we make a T-shirt and list them on the front and back so we'd always be reminded of them. I told everyone I thought that was a clever idea. But I also thought we needed something else in writing, and that's when I came up with the idea of the Values Questionnaire that would be filled out on a quarterly basis. That way people could really have a tangible, visual account of how well we were meeting our objectives. I told them we could rate ourselves on a scale of one to five, one meaning "needs improvement" and five meaning we were doing a great job. These are the values that we would include on the questionnaire:

The FineFax Core Values

The Values We Want	What We Do to Get Them
1. High Quality	• Build continuous improvement through immediate feedback
	• Develop ownership and pride
	• Stay proactive, not reactive
	• Continuously evolve toward exceeding customer expectations
	• Assure survival by aiming for perfection
2. Customer Satisfaction	• Always respond beyond customer expectations
	• Provide a complete and immediate response to customer concerns
	• Empower teams to make decisions to satisfy customers

3. Leadership
- Lead by example
- Develop sensitivity
- Maintain credibility, integrity, and honesty
- Be a motivator, catalyst, and coach
- Keep the sense of urgency alive

4. Risk Taking and Innovation
- Exceed expectations
- Dare to be different
- Never accept mediocrity
- Learn from failure
- Have the courage to take an unpopular view
- Foster change

5. People Development
- Give sincere and immediate constructive feedback and recognition
- Provide career development and support
- Identify weaknesses and strengths
- Develop across-job descriptions
- Encourage self-development

6. Teamwork
- Focus on a common purpose
- Eliminate territorial barriers
- Build "win-win" relationships with team members
- Emphasize honesty and trust
- Maintain open communications with all levels in the company
- Stay flexible

I read through the values we had defined. I was sold. The linkage between vision, business objectives, and core values made so much sense to me that right then and there I switched from agnostic to earnest disciple and proposed that this vision statement process be added to our growing list of Unmanagement Principles.

We were a pretty self-satisfied group, sitting there, pleased with our accomplishment, amid empty pizza boxes and soda cans. In fact, we even thought we had the strength left to make an attempt at getting back to the original purpose that had convened this group in the first place. We were wrong, but we gave it a good try anyway. There wasn't much interest in going over my "Kansas" speech, but we did take a stab at figuring out how to implement the Unmanagement principles I'd identified because it seemed like so much of a no-brainer. I mean, when we asked ourselves "Who will carry out the principles?" there really was only one possible answer — the team. And to make sure there was no mistaking that fact, we enshrined our commitment to the team approach in the following timeless prose:

Business Teams

At the heart of the workplace transformation is a firm belief in and support of the team concept, democratic team functioning, and participatory decision making. The business team is thus the cornerstone on which the entire organization is constructed.

The business team itself is understood to be a small, autonomous work group empowered by supporting changes in vision, expectation, objectives, and business systems — all of which encourage and reinforce participation, teamwork, understanding, and commitment to a single goal.

But then we lost it completely. There were other significant questions about teams still to be answered, such as: How would they be formed? Who would be on them? How would they get their work done? But we had to put them off to another day because we were simply too exhausted to think about it anymore.

The next morning I had a voice-mail message from Treddle. It was as if he had been in the room with us the day before. He reminded me that I had fewer than 45 days to come up with some results and that having highbrow principles was all well and good, but he was looking for bottom-line profits. I don't know if he meant to intimidate me or discourage me, but I wasn't buying into it. We had come too far to turn back now. We were really just getting started.

Chapter Nine

SEEING IS BELIEVING

If your business is anything like FineFax was, by the time you get around to introducing Unmanagement, employees will have already been subjected to a variety of quality improvement programs and corporate "feel-good" campaigns. And since so few of these programs ever seem to go anywhere, employees will naturally be highly skeptical of what they'll see as just another pointless waste of time. For this reason, I think it's extremely important to make what we call "visual commitments to change" as soon as possible.

I don't remember exactly who came up with that expression. As I recall, it grew out of an informal discussion among some managers and employees not long after my "Kansas" speech. The managers were going on about how Unmanagement would make for some radical changes around FineFax, and the employees were saying that they'd be waiting to see if management would really "walk the walk and talk the talk" this time. By the time I got included in the loop, the idea had progressed to the point where management should make some "sign" of its intentions, and that soon led to the full concept of "visual commitments to change."

So what, you rightly wonder, are they? In our definition, a visual commitment is any action, sign, symbol, event, or behavior that announces not only that Unmanagement is under way, but also that the company supports it wholeheartedly. The actual types of commitments you can use are limited only by your imagination, but there is one essential principle to follow:

Vital Visuals

Any sincere, visual commitment to change is good but the best are always those that tear down the barriers between managers and employees.

Interestingly, one of the best visuals we ever made at FineFax happened without our being aware of it. In retrospect, the rotation of groups during my "Kansas" speech was more than an effective way to meet the entire population. It was also a major visual commitment to change. Not only had such a thing never been done before, but it also struck at one of the most imposing barriers of them all, namely, communication. Most traditional corporations, and FineFax was no exception, carefully control information of all kinds — particularly information about the company's sales, expenses, and profits. In short, management gets information and the employees do not, and that in turn reduces the employees' sense of ownership in the company, as well as their commitment to its success. The "Kansas" meetings announced in a way that everybody could see that from now on everybody would be in on the important facts.

Of course, once we identified visuals for what they were, we developed a little more conscious control over their use. For example, continuing with our new open-communication theme, we set up "Information Centers" at several locations in the plant. They were simple, cloth-covered folding wall panels, but they included exhibits that had never been publicly displayed on the production floor. In fact, the walls were intentionally covered with charts that would enable employees to visually track each one of our six main business objectives, such as the rise and fall of both quality and customer service complaints.

We also adopted a "dress-down" code stating that no one in the plant had to wear coats and ties anymore unless they were escorting customers visiting the plant on business, and even then, only if the customers were known to be put off by unconventional business attire.

In addition, crews were sent out immediately to clean and paint the plant with the specific intention of eliminating the physical impression that not only were managers and employees living in two different worlds, but also that real estate in the employees' world simply wasn't worth as much.

And there were other visual commitments to change on the way. In fact, one of the most sensational took place only a month or so later when employees were told they could determine their own break times rather than wait like Pavlov's dogs for the horn to sound, as they had previously done. This particular adjustment to the normal order of things at FineFax created so much anxiety among the managers that first I had to form a small task force, headed by Rachel Lindenmeyer from human resources, to study its feasibility. But two weeks passed and not a word from Rachel. So I asked her to stop by my office.

"What's up, Rachel?" I said. "I haven't heard from you. Are we going through with this or not?"

"Well, we're still studying it," she said. "This is a very radical change, and we want to be sure it will work."

"Rachel, I want you to know I appreciate your concern and all the work you've done, but I think the only way we're ever going to know if it works is to try it and see what happens. I think we should start tomorrow. What do you say?"

"But there's going to be chaos," she said. "They're just not ready for this. It's too much too fast."

"Aw c'mon, Rachel," I said. "Everything will be fine."

Truth was, though, I was almost as worried as Rachel. And the next day when the usual break time came around, I was in my office biting my nails just like the other managers. But the experiment was a great success. Not only did the employees choose their break times intelligently, but also they made sure their work areas were staffed properly to keep production moving along in the meantime.

Sometimes that's what you have to do: Ready! Fire! Aim!

Chapter Ten

LEADERSHIP

Not long after the first effects of Unmanagement had made their way throughout the plant, I sat down with six employees from the production floor for an informal discussion about how Unmanagement seemed to be taking hold.

The news was not good.

The employees said that although their supervisors all seemed to talk about Unmanagement as a great idea, they didn't seem particularly eager to use Unmanagement in practice. That revelation left me more than a little confused because, whenever I talked with the supervisors myself, I always came away convinced they were strong supporters of the new program.

So the next day, I met with all the supervisors to ask them about their commitment directly.

"Yes, indeed," they all said. "Absolutely. Behind it 100 percent. Absolutely."

But I was not reassured. For example, when the supervisors were all pledging their support, many were not looking directly at me but at their friends with a conspiratorial, sidelong glance. In addition, there was an undertone to their answers that seemed to be saying: "Are you kidding? What do you think we are — nuts?"

"I really need you to be honest with me now," I said. "Are you being honest with me?"

The supervisors mumbled and shifted around in their chairs and glanced at their buddies some more, but there was no definite answer to the question.

"Well," I said, "if you're not being honest with me, that must mean we've got a problem with trust here. So let me ask you this. Does everybody trust everybody else in this room? Can I see a show of hands?"

All the supervisors raised their hands.

"You know," I said, "maybe a better way to answer that question would be for us all to write down our answers anonymously on a slip of paper and then see what we come up with."

And do you know what? When I looked through the results, "no" had been written on every paper. I looked up at the supervisors and said, "I think we're in a little bit of trouble here."

"It's clear enough," I said, "that we really don't trust each other, so let me ask you a question and let's start with me, 'Why don't you trust me? How can I be better at my job?'"

Over the next couple hours, the supervisors gave me a look at myself as the plant's foremost leader from their point of view. One supervisor said that I was not a good listener, that I often seemed so preoccupied with some agenda of my own design that I shut out ideas from anyone else. Another agreed and pointed out that during one-on-one discussions in my office, I had the disconcerting habit of taking phone calls and speed-reading the mail in my in-box. Most of the comments, though, centered on what they said was my "conflicting" management style. "You give mixed signals," a supervisor said. "Sometimes you want us to act independently, but other times you want to run everything yourself."

In the beginning of this first Truth and Honesty Session, I was the center of attention, but as the session progressed, an important change took place. "You know," a supervisor said after listening to the group discuss my mixed signals, "I think I do that, too." The supervisor almost blurted it out as if the observation had taken him by surprise. But once said, it opened the door to other similar insights as the supervisors began to examine their own individual approaches to leadership and management. To me that meant they were developing a personal sense of ownership in the process.

There were several times during these proceedings when I wished I hadn't gotten into them in the first place, but when the supervisors began to talk about themselves, I was more confident that we were headed in the right direction. At the end of the meeting, I promised that in the days ahead I would try to improve my listening skills, as well as resolve the split in my managerial personality. And if they caught me at either one, I said, I wanted them to point it out to me.

Overall, the group found the Truth and Honesty Session so helpful that after a while they worked up a set of guidelines so the sessions could be used throughout the plant.

The Truth and Honesty Session at Work

- Truth and Honesty Sessions can be used at all levels of management. General managers get together with their staffs, middle managers meet with their staffs, and supervisors meet with employees. The program works best if the general manager goes first and sets an example.

- Each session begins by focusing on one individual. That individual should listen to the comments and take notes but should not try to refute or rebut any of the comments. Arguments are counterproductive because if the person expects a fight, the other participants will not be likely to contribute.

- Truth and Honesty Sessions are not adversarial or confrontational. The participants must support one another and help each other identify "opportunities for personal improvement." Any constructive criticism must always come with a specific example. Unfounded speculations are not helpful.

- In the second part of every Truth and Honesty Session, the participants should turn their attention inward. They should examine the opportunities for improvement that they have just drawn up for the person who has been the main focus of the session and identify those that may apply to themselves.

- The person who has been the focus of the meeting should commit to work on a specific development opportunity.

- Follow-up meetings should be scheduled at realistic intervals, say, every three months, as part of a routine staff meeting. The follow-ups will serve as "calibration checks" for the person who was the original subject of the session. Simply asking someone how he or she is doing on your way to the cafeteria is not a bad idea either.

Of course, all of us at the meeting realized there was something unique about the situation we found ourselves in, if only because we felt so uncomfortable. But there was more to it than that. While it was certainly true that trust was in short supply, that lack of trust, as the group would soon learn, was in fact symptomatic of a larger problem: FineFax's leaders — its managers and supervisors — were not leading effectively. And it wasn't for lack of trying. These leaders were simply at an enormous disadvantage because they were still under the influence of traditional leadership patterns that had grown increasingly obsolete.

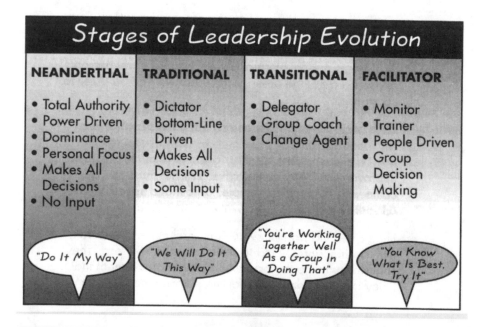

Stages of Leadership Evolution

NEANDERTHAL	TRADITIONAL	TRANSITIONAL	FACILITATOR
• Total Authority	• Dictator	• Delegator	• Monitor
• Power Driven	• Bottom-Line	• Group Coach	• Trainer
• Dominance	Driven	• Change Agent	• People Driven
• Personal Focus	• Makes All		• Group
• Makes All	Decisions		Decision
Decisions	• Some Input		Making
• No Input			
"Do It My Way"	"We Will Do It This Way"	"You're Working Together Well As a Group In Doing That"	"You Know What Is Best. Try It"

As subsequent events at FineFax would show, the very idea of what constitutes good leadership undergoes a profound transformation when a company adopts Unmanagement. In many ways, I think it resembles the theory of evolution. For example, I see four distinct stages beginning with the "Neanderthal Manager," a prehistoric life form still common in corporate America, and ending with the "Future Facilitator," the advanced management species of tomorrow. As managers reach each more advanced level of evolutionary development, they become better and better leaders because they're sharing more and more responsibility with employees. Neanderthals, for example, share none, whereas Future Facilitators encourage widespread employee involvement in running the business. In addition, at each level managers possess different characteristics and even talk to employees differently.

The leadership transformation is also like evolution for another reason — neither one is an overnight phenomenon. It's never easy to break old habits, and you'll have to accept that changing your leadership techniques will take time and practice. Nonetheless, at FineFax we did find seven qualities of effective leadership that you can start on right away.

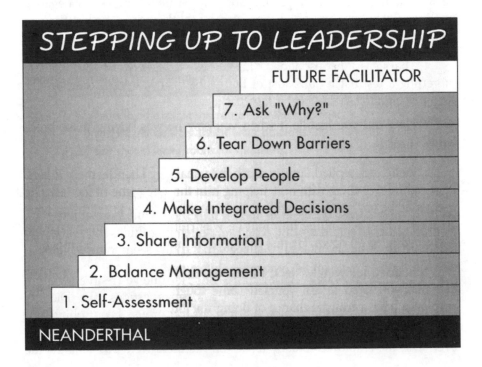

STEPPING UP TO LEADERSHIP

FUTURE FACILITATOR

7. Ask "Why?"

6. Tear Down Barriers

5. Develop People

4. Make Integrated Decisions

3. Share Information

2. Balance Management

1. Self-Assessment

NEANDERTHAL

So, let's say traditional managers want to become Unmanagers. What do they have to do in order to climb those leadership steps successfully? Let me tell you a story about our materials manager, Jack Johnson. What can I say about Jack, except that he was not the type of manager to whom people would want to tell their problems. Concerned about letting people know who was boss, Jack very much fell into the Neanderthal Manager category. After knowing Jack for a while, I decided it would be my personal mission to help transform him into a Future Facilitator. I systematically went through each of the seven qualities of effective leadership and helped Jack to attain these qualities, using a variety of techniques. It was remarkable how he was able to climb up the evolutionary ladder to Future Facilitator in only a very short time. Here's how he did it.

Self-Assessment

As our resident guinea pig, Jack started out by listing out loud what he thought was his own management style. He mentioned several positive qualities: responsible, consistent, thorough, but as he went through the list, he was having a hard time pinpointing any particular quirks or negative qualities. So, to help him out, I suggested he think back to the last time an employee disappointed him.

"That's easy," he responded. "Last week we were over two hours late in getting a test batch out. Most of the problems came from Tom Weaver, who just couldn't seem to get it together."

"How did you handle it when you saw he was having these problems?" I asked.

"Well," Jack replied, "pretty much the usual way I handle these things. I got right down there with him, helping him through some of the tasks he seemed to be having trouble with. It took us quite a while to get things back on track. I kept reminding him that he was ruining things for everybody and slowing us all down. He just shrugged. It didn't seem to help much."

I nodded knowingly. "Jack, I think the next time you're in a situation like this, you need to ask yourself some tough questions, like 'Did the employee have a realistic chance of doing the job, or was I controlling and interfering too often?' or 'Was I dictating commitment or inspiring it?' or even 'Did the employee actually try to tell me there were problems on the job, but I just wasn't listening?' These are all issues a facilitator will have to grapple with." Someone suggested we conduct a Truth and Honesty Session with Jack, which actually went very well and brought up a lot of issues all of us needed to examine more carefully. But let's move on to the next step.

Balance Management

The next step is balance management. Jack was having a lot of trouble adjusting to this step of the process, but it is a bit tricky, so who can blame him? Basically, as an Unmanager, you have to learn how to balance giving up control with taking charge. Jack, being the kind of manager who spent a large part of his career dictating orders to employees, told us he didn't quite know how to sit back and cheer on his workers. Luckily, we set him straight. After all, balance management doesn't mean becoming a virtual cheerleader. Quite the contrary! As we pointed out to him, his role now was to learn how to take charge in a different way. He needed to learn how to create a distinction between a request and a dictate. Dictates deny individual competence while requests recognize and encourage it. Obviously, requests are always much better. In order to change a dictate into a request, three things have to happen:

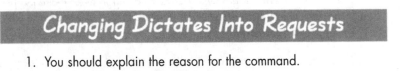

Changing Dictates Into Requests

1. You should explain the reason for the command.
2. You should actively solicit other opinions.
3. You should leave room for questions.

For example, I told Jack that it's one thing to tell someone to "Turn off the lights" during a presentation and let it go at that. But it's quite another, and far better, to say to that same person, "Would you turn off the lights because we're about to start a slide show and, by the way, if you think that leaves the room too dark, do you have another idea?" I'm oversimplifying here, but I'm sure you get the idea.

Well, Jack tried it, and believe me, it took a whole lot of practice before he started getting the hang of it. He went through so many changes that another manager (with probably too much time on her hands) actually put together what she called "The Tate Family." Here then, is a mini-bio of all the family members.

The Tate Family

1. **Dictate.** The founding father of the family who is known for barking out orders, a total authoritarian, and very power driven. He tells everyone what to do. It's either his way or the highway.

2. **Potentate.** Dictate's wife. She still acts like a queen, but now at least she's invited some of the staff to join her court. She tries to integrate people into positions of authority. And because she brings in a few more people, the overall quality of the decisions being made improves.

3. **Hesitate.** Dictate's uncertain younger brother. He tries to integrate a few people, but still hesitates over whether or not he should be like Dictate. He is ambivalent and asks, "When do I give orders and when do I not? When do I let people figure things out for themselves and when do I step in?" He has noted the good results Potentate got and wants to bring in even more people. But he has a little identity crisis and is confused about the role he's supposed to assume.

4. **Irritate.** Hesitate's wife. When she works closely with him, she gets upset. She'll ask him, "Well, how am I supposed to do this job?" And he answers, "Well, I'm not really sure. How do you think you should be doing it?"

5. **Mediate.** The wise grandfather of Dictate. He waits until teams come together and often mediates situations as the teams learn how to arrive at a consensus on their own.

6. **Facilitate.** The wife of Mediate, known mostly as a coach and trainer who uses requests and no dictating at all. She's interested in people development, not control.

Even the best coaches in professional sports must occasionally take direct control of the team's activities. Similarly, Unmanagers must also realize that there will be crises and other times when they, too, must take charge of their teams. Indeed, employees will expect it. The trick here is to balance one's management style to accommodate those moments while avoiding either extreme.

Jack was ultimately able to be a lot better about facilitating his employees, rather than taking over for them. In fact, he learned that Tom Weaver was just the sort of person who needed to be given less direction, not more. Now, when Jack sees Tom is falling behind, he asks how he can best help Tom get back on track, and then he waits for Tom to direct him.

Share Information

Traditionally, managers have used the control of information to maintain their power base within their own personal fiefdoms. In addition, the control of information lies at the heart of what creates the "two different worlds" between managers and employees. This control is like the Berlin Wall. When it's in place, no one can get beyond it but when it begins to come down, it can unite a company.

Originally, when we told Jack he needed to start sharing information more with his employees in order to become a model Unmanager, he seemed a bit perplexed.

"I honestly have to think about that," he told me. "I mean, I feel like I share information with people one-on-one, but there must be a way to expand my scope." Later on, when we revisited this topic, Jack seemed excited and told me he had discovered the perfect forum in which to change the way information is shared throughout the company.

"The way I see it," he said, "to truly share information across the board at FineFax, we should hold meetings that include subjects we don't usually cover and invite guests we don't normally invite. For example," he went on, "all those staff meetings we have on Monday mornings for the department heads are pretty bad for employee morale. They create an 'Us vs. Them' mentality."

"I see where you're going," said Marie McCormick, a fellow worker in the materials department. "If we include employees from other departments with related concerns, we just might hack away at that elitist mentality. I can see our department inviting people from the production area.

Or the engineering department could invite someone from the materials group."

"Exactly," Jack said. He was getting kind of excited by this idea and he began tapping his pen up and down on his notepad. "Or take the monthly departmental meetings that involve all the people in a given functional area and not just managers and supervisors. What if, in addition to inviting guests to these meetings, we broaden the content of the meetings to share information more widely?"

"What do you mean?" Marie asked.

"Well, most departmental meetings traditionally focus on specific in-house business issues, but you can use them for many other purposes," he replied. "Training is a good case in point. If you've recently seen a particularly good videotape on the latest leadership techniques in corporate America, for example, the departmental meeting would be a perfect time to share that tape with the rest of the department. "

"And we could invite customers to our quarterly general plant meetings," I chimed in. "The customer could serve as the meeting's keynote speaker. People in the plant will have been hearing a lot about customers and the importance of customer service, and this would be a perfect chance to let them interact with the real thing. The dialogue can be especially meaningful because the employees can hear an honest appraisal of our plant's customer service directly from the customer's point of view."

We all looked at each other and I could see by everyone's animated expressions that we had discovered something pretty important: In general, sharing information increases the knowledge of everyone in a plant or office, which in turn can only improve your business. And it's also a highly visible commitment to change. Unmanagers in the making should always remember that everyone in the plant needs to experience the excitement of new intellectual discoveries just as much as they do. It's exactly this kind of sharing that creates the momentum Unmanagement needs to succeed.

By that point we were all pretty exhausted and decided to call it a day. We would continue our discussion of how to become a Future Facilitator the following morning and try to guide Jack through the remainder of the steps he needed to climb out of his cave.

Chapter Eleven

THE DEATH OF
A PRIMATE

The next morning, Jack walked into the brainstorming room nearly bursting. He seemed invigorated, as if all along there was another Jack hiding inside, waiting to pop out. He told us he could barely sleep because all these new ideas had been churning around inside his head. He had been thinking a lot about the discoveries we had made about sharing information and suggested we take these ideas a whole lot further.

"Give us an example," I suggested.

"Well, it occurred to me over breakfast this morning," he said. "When my wife and I make decisions regarding family matters, we've started to include our teenage son and daughter in the discussions. They've gotten to an age where what we decide affects them — you know, financial matters, family vacation, things like that. And I just thought that this all-inclusive philosophy could also be practiced more within the company."

It was a brilliant notion and as soon as he said it, other managers in the room added their two cents to the discussion. Soon we had all agreed on a new FineFax practice. We called it the "Art of Making Integrated Decisions."

Make Integrated Decisions

It may sound like something out of "Ripley's Believe It or Not," but it is true that managers often hold meetings and make decisions on issues without inviting any of the people who know the most about the subject. It isn't at all uncommon to see managers meeting on quality without any of the quality people in attendance, or on human resources without any of the human resources people there. Needless to say, this does not constitute effective leadership, and it's not the Unmanagement way.

Jack decided to issue a proclamation. He made a big production out of it, sweeping around the room as if he were a court messenger, sharing his edict with the masses. When you come right down to it, Jack could be a bit of a ham, but then again, so could I.

"I hereby decree," he announced, "that as Unmanagers, we will no longer make decisions in a vacuum; instead, we will integrate decision making, both horizontally to include different functional areas and vertically to include senior managers, supervisors, and employees."

Everybody applauded and Jack took a deep bow. Someone asked where he parked his horse, and a few people started to giggle.

Thinking about it later, it occurred to me that integrated decision making boiled down to a three-part process of setting business objectives, budgeting, and communications. Early on in any new Unmanagement program, the different functional areas of a company should be learning the importance of coordinating their objectives. For example, it's unrealistic for the production department to set production goals without involving the materials department because the two of them need to agree, for instance, on inventory requirements.

But that collaboration can extend even further to include collaborative budgeting. Typically, traditional managers will instruct each functional area to submit a budget, and then all the various individual budgets are combined into one package at the most senior levels of management. But in Unmanagement, overall results will be much better if the final integration starts long before it ever reaches senior management. Consider a plant manager who is struggling to set the annual budget for employee training; it would be much better to involve production supervisors in the process as early as possible. More than likely, the supervisors would be able to come up with a plan to share training resources that would be more productive and cost-effective than any budget the plant manager could work up alone.

Although there are many benefits to integrated decision making, they will only be realized if the collaborative process is supported by the right communication system. Of course, that would fall under the "Share Information" category that Jack hammered out earlier.

Develop People

Developing people, the next task of a Future Facilitator, was one Jack really needed to explore. Probably the best way to describe how he changed in this area is to tell you the story of Luann and the great meeting fiasco.

Luann's Great Mistake

Luann was one of Jack's employees, and she was given the responsibility of communicating some of the finer points of testing equipment to several department heads at a plant meeting. Trouble was, Luann wasn't too experienced at presenting information, and when she got up to speak, she choked.

As everyone sat there, waiting to hear her speak, she sputtered, turned several shades of red, and finally managed to croak out, "Well, there are many different areas to cover, and I'd like to turn the meeting over to John, here, who can explain a few."

Luckily, John was more experienced at this sort of thing and was able to take over while Luann regained her composure. After the meeting was over, you can imagine poor Neanderthal Jack was furious. But because we had been practicing Unmanagement, instead of talking with Luann directly, he came into my office first.

"Okay, Trish," he said, "what would an Unmanager do in this situation?"

"Well, do you value Luann as an employee, Jack?" I asked him.

He answered enthusiastically that, yes, she had been an outstanding employee so far.

"If so, and if you see a great deal of potential in her, then you need to treat her as though she's capable of correcting her own mistakes. Put her in charge of resolving her own dilemmas. Unmanage her by asking her what *she* wants to do about this."

He nodded knowingly. This Unmanagement stuff was really starting to sink in. The next day I got a call from Jack.

"Well," he told me, "when Luann came into my office, I sat her down. She looked like she was about to get struck by a torpedo, practically cowering next to my desk. I just looked at her and said, 'Gee, Luann, what do you think about what happened yesterday?' She told me that she had gotten nervous and started to apologize profusely, but I stopped her. I told her that I respected her and knew that she could do a good job and asked her to tell me what she thought was the best way to handle this situation. She looked at me a little stunned. I tried not to smile, but, Trish, it was pretty funny how surprised she looked.

"Then she said, 'Well, I guess I would want to work on practicing my public speaking. Maybe I could join a local Toastmasters group and brush up my presentation skills.' I told her I thought that was a fine idea and she got up, still uncertain about exactly what I was up to, and walked out of my office."

Jack was surprised at how effective this technique was, but gradually, as Unmanagement started to take hold at FineFax, he and the other managers began to understand. Our success depended not on their jealously guarding the boundaries of their fiefdoms, but on developing the skills and knowledge of other people at all levels of the company.

Ultimately, there came a time at FineFax when the Unmanagers thought developing people was so important to the ultimate success of Unmanagement, they institutionalized it as a separate program of universal education, which they called "Operation Egghead." One of the great triumphs of the FineFax experience (which I'll describe in detail later),

Egghead offered employees training in all kinds of subjects, including job skills, business knowledge, interpersonal skills, and ethics and values.

Tear Down Barriers

Part of developing people includes removing the obstacles of needless privileges, perquisites, and status symbols that have traditionally separated managers and employees. We held several brainstorming sessions on this one, and everyone contributed suggestions until we finally came up with what I consider to be a pretty comprehensive list. We called them "Barrier Busters" and put them up where Unmanagers could be reminded of them.

Barrier Busters

1. **Practice what you preach.** Eliminate executive perks, such as reserved parking for managers and the executive dining room. Try letting other people use your office for meetings.

2. **Admit mistakes.** It is critical that you openly admit a mistake or a poor decision. Then discuss what you've learned because every time you do, you're setting a powerful example for employees.

(By the way, this one was a doozie. Curtis Billup, a production supervisor on the second shift, really set the standard for this. When one of his team members failed to calibrate his test equipment and then failed to detect dozens of bad circuit boards, Curtis went out to the line and started hollering at the guy. But Curtis caught himself. He cooled off for a while and came back and said to the employee, "Look, I'd like to apologize for hollering that way. I know it was a mistake and that you didn't mean to do it. I want to help you so it doesn't happen again. Tell me what you think went wrong here, and let me help get the circuit boards over to the repair people." That was a proud moment.)

3. **Allow disagreements.** Help people feel comfortable giving other viewpoints. Clearly outline that you expect disagreement and value other viewpoints. Your reactions when people present a dissenting opinion will be critical. Listen to it carefully, thank them for the input, ask other people if they feel the same way, and if they do, start negotiating a solution.

4. **Solicit ideas.** Before ending any meeting or finalizing any decision, always make sure to ask for additional suggestions. Listen carefully and be available for employees at all times.

5. **Take action.** Whenever an employee suggestion has been adopted, managers must always follow it up with visible action. Anything less will be seen as a sign that suggestions are not taken seriously, and employees will soon stop giving them.

Ask "Why?"

The final test, the true mark that Jack had crossed the threshold into the realm of Future Facilitator occurred a couple days after we put up the Barrier Busters list. If you'll remember, Jack is the guy who likes to give orders. Confident, a bit brash, and very authoritative, he was the last person you'd expect to solicit advice. Well, if I hadn't witnessed it myself, I wouldn't believe it, but Jack actually started coming to work and asking people questions.

It may seem inconsequential, but this final attribute of effective leadership is one of the most productive of them all. Too often people do their jobs over and over again in the same ways, never once asking why something is done one way and not another. Obviously, when there's no curiosi-

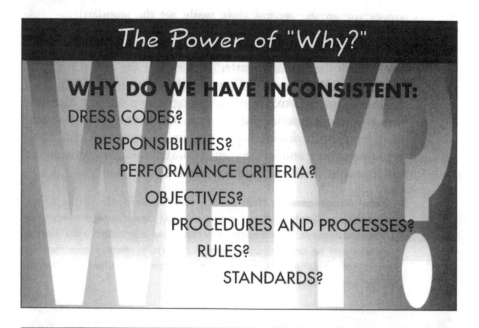

The Power of "Why?"

WHY DO WE HAVE INCONSISTENT:

DRESS CODES?

RESPONSIBILITIES?

PERFORMANCE CRITERIA?

OBJECTIVES?

PROCEDURES AND PROCESSES?

RULES?

STANDARDS?

ty, there will also be no change made for the better. Asking "why" breaks this cycle and opens the door to innovation, particularly in the area of breaking down barriers between managers and employees.

Jack soon discovered that by asking why about everything and anything at least three times a day, he uncovered questions that otherwise might not have come to light. What's more, a by-product of all his questions was that by asking people for their opinions, he was asking those people to think, and the more people are asked to think, the more they are going to think on their own. Pretty soon everyone at the plant was starting to ask questions and challenge old assumptions. I can't believe how far-reaching this technique became at the plant. Even the delivery people started examining their own methods and habits. It was quite a sight to behold!

When the day came for Jack to be acknowledged for his fine transformation into a full-fledged Unmanager, I called a small group of people into my office. I had ordered a few snacks and some sodas. After everyone got settled, I stood up and announced that we had gathered together to honor a great thing: the evolution of a Neanderthal Manager into a Future Facilitator. As people clapped, I brought out a giant picture of an ape pounding its chest. "Here, Jack. Something to remind you of how far you've come." He was pretty good-natured about the whole thing. He just grinned and told me he was surprised his wife was able to dig up such an old photo from the family album. Then we all had a good laugh, and a few people came up to congratulate him personally.

I started thinking about how Walter Treddle himself would be impressed, had he been there. I had a little more than a month left to prove myself to him, and I was feeling more confident about my chances. On the other hand, I wouldn't be surprised if Walter already somehow knew what was going on. That seemed to be the regular state of affairs these days.

That about covers how we went about improving leadership, the first area I discussed in my "Kansas" speech that we were going to tackle. But there is one final note I would like to add. Although most of what I have just been talking about has concerned itself with the details of leadership, I would like to explain that this whole matter of leadership change is itself based on an even more generic principle of major importance to Unmanagement:

Managers often assume that adopting Unmanagement means that only employees must redefine their roles and that it is the manager's job to help them do it. In fact, Unmanagement requires that employees and managers both redefine their roles.

Chapter Twelve

PROCESS, TEAMS, AND "ERGONOMIC" DAVE

The time had come to take on the FineFax production line. When I had first seen that line, I knew in my gut that improving its processes — the way work was being done on the line — would be very important to the success or failure of our whole Unmanagement experiment. Besides, it was the second area in my speech that I wanted to tackle. But I was still surprised to find out just how right my hunch had been when we actually got started on the project.

While the undertaking produced results that were more or less expected, such as increasing the plant's productivity, it also inspired breakthroughs that I found nothing short of startling. In changing processes we learned the secret of creating teams. And here we also learned that to successfully change a process required a whole new concept of how process changes were supposed to relate to the human beings they affected. If that wasn't enough, the undertaking also gave us our first, who-would-ever-have-thought, "Hero of Unmanagement."

That changing the line's processes would turn out to have such profound, hidden consequences was all the more surprising because, at the start, the project appeared to be little more than a straightforward, mechanical exercise in applied engineering and materials management. The FineFax line was a conventional, linear production line that changed between three different fax models, and each model moved through specific assembly and testing procedures. But this line, you will recall, had a big problem. Between the various steps in assembly and testing, work in process had to be temporarily inventoried in a large holding cage, and this bottleneck hurt the line's overall productivity.

So the FineFax engineers were called in to study this predicament, and they concluded that the bottleneck had two causes. First, scheduling the arrival of parts to the production line was not well coordinated. As a result, fax units sat idle in the cage waiting for the right parts to show up. Second, work in process also had to be stored in the cage because the testers were unable to keep up with the line's output.

Clearly, the initial objective here was to reduce or eliminate the need to inventory fax units in process between steps in the manufacturing process. And not to worry, said engineering, solutions were close at hand. They would work with materials management and improve the scheduling of parts to the line by installing Just-in-Time inventory management techniques. Then they would either put more people into equipment and testing, or they would balance out the line's production schedule so that assemblers could stop making product at a certain point and help out in testing.

Everyone was pleased with engineering's plan. It was practical and it did promise results.

Then Dave Polanski had his brainstorm.

That event altered the way people worked at FineFax, both on the line and everywhere else, far beyond anything that I or anybody else had yet imagined, and it demonstrated conclusively that our approach to changing the production process needed a whole new conceptual foundation. Conventional thinking was no longer good enough. Dave's revelation hit FineFax with a jolt. Not only was his idea sufficiently striking in itself, but also Dave was the last person you'd have guessed would have come up with it.

Dave was a complex character, misunderstood by almost everyone he worked with, largely because he chose to give them no alternative. He was very concerned about his image and worked overtime to project himself as an "engineer's engineer," a man who dealt with mathematical fact and scientific precision. But if the truth were told, Dave was as softhearted a man as anyone could ever hope to meet. Even though he was a bit awkward with emotions and feelings — hardly the stuff of exact science anyway — Dave was nonetheless intensely interested in working with the production people as people and not merely as symbols on some engineering process chart. Too often, he felt, engineering ended up proposing changes that were better suited to textbooks than they were to addressing the needs of real people. Unfortunately, he worried that his point of view might be seen as something unbecoming his professional station at the plant. To make sure that never happened, Dave often ended up overcompensating in some way to show that he was properly distant and coolly scientific. In fact, it was just such a reaction that had caused him to charge into my office that day brandishing his employment contract and raving that nowhere did it say he had to talk to people. Not surprisingly, Dave Polanski was regarded as a bit "cold" around FineFax — definitely not a "people person."

Although he struggled mightily to maintain his pose, Dave couldn't help revealing his true colors sooner or later. He'd been puzzling for years over how to invest process changes with a more human touch. One day he was bound to figure it out. And that day finally arrived when — just as his own department's recommendations were about to be implemented on the production line — Dave was compelled to abandon his charade entirely by an especially penetrating insight that at last showed him the missing link between process change and human need.

Dave, I learned later, had been talking with two production line employees when he made the intuitive leap that in turn made him famous. The employees had just remarked in an offhand way that communication on the line wasn't so hot because often when the line changed out to a new fax model, the people in the test section at the back of the line didn't know that the model type had changed. Therefore, they were still using settings for the previous model when the new ones arrived. And they said they couldn't understand why something simple like a flashing yellow light couldn't be installed in a conspicuous place to let everyone know when the line was changing. And that's when Dave discovered his dictum.

Dave's Dictum

The primary objective of changes to production processes of any kind in any business should be to increase communication and feedback between the people actually doing the work so they get relevant information as fast as possible. Without this linkage to a human context, process change exists in a vacuum and cannot be expected to achieve lasting value.

Viewed against this backdrop, it was clear to Dave that the changes about to be put in place on the line did not have the right objective in mind; that is, they did not increase communication and feedback. Things like Just-in-Time inventory control were still excellent and necessary ideas, but they were obviously meant to be parts of some larger strategy that would be based on communication. As Dave pondered what that new strategy might be, he began to see the production line from a new point of view. On all the production lines he had known, communication and feedback for the employees took place only between the employees and the supervisor. What's more, because of the fiefdom mentality in most corporations, supervisors rarely communicated with more than one specific group of employees, and the employees on the line rarely had any organized way of communicating with each other. The FineFax line was an excellent case in point. At FineFax, all the assembly people spoke only with the assembly supervisor, and all the test people spoke only with the test supervisor. There was little, if any, interaction between the two groups.

At this point, Dave realized that he didn't know how to proceed. The communication pattern on the line was such an accepted part of American business and had been in place for so long that it was difficult to see beyond it; it was like figuring out how to break a bad habit. Dave turned to his colleagues, other Unmanagers in the making, for help. Although they embraced Dave's Dictum enthusiastically, they, too, were unable to implement it effectively on the line. But then one of the Unmanagers suggested that this problem was really an opportunity to demonstrate the power of their new Unmanagement philosophy. After all, hadn't they been saying all along that their whole approach was based on the conviction that employees could and should be much more involved in actually running a business, that managers were nuts if they continued to think they had to do everything by themselves? Clearly, this Unmanager said, here was a great time to get the employees involved. Ask them how to change the line so it will conform to Dave's Dictum.

That inspiration produced one of the proudest moments in the history of Unmanagement at FineFax. The employees, working with the managers, came up with a great strategy that also had profound implications for the whole theory and practice of Unmanagement.

Using cutout plastic templates representing various features of their work environment, the employees designed a totally new arrangement for the line. In the past, the line had built up its inventory. Then eventually, someone would take all the circuit packs out of the stockroom and put together a fax machine. Then someone else would bring it to the testers for inspection. If the machine failed the test, the tester would say, "Someone assembled this part wrong." But by then, two years might have passed between the time the product was made and the time it was tested. That made it hard for anyone to learn from past mistakes.

The employees decided that the line needed to be configured differently. They broke up the one line into three separate production "modules," one for each of FineFax's three different fax models. Within each module, they included all the people who worked directly on that model — that is, both assembly and test people.

Under the old arrangement, assemblers reported to one supervisor and testers to another with little or no interaction between the two supervisory groups; however, under the new design, assemblers and testers in each module all talked directly to the supervisor for that module. Then, each week, representatives from each of the three modules would get together to make sure that all the production employees, no matter what group they were in, would all be reading from the same page. This type of cross-module familiarity was important because employees working in each of the modules would be expected to help out making any of the other fax models if the need arose.

And last, but certainly not least, the employees' plan finally eliminated the holding cages because each module would also feature the earlier changes devised by the Unmanagers, including Just-in-Time inventory management and more test equipment. Although I may seem to be glossing over the Just-in-Time method, I really believe it, or one of the other similar approaches in use today, will be critical to your Unmanagement program. It's just that tons of books have been written on these inventory techniques, and you would be better off getting the details from them.

We now had a new structure for the line that everyone could start building immediately, and that wasn't the only benefit. As we analyzed the new structure and discussed the reasoning behind it, we were also able to identify several generic principles that could be used in the future and that, along with Dave's Dictum, became essential parts of Unmanagement.

The first principle, and probably the most obvious, was:

> 1. *Always involve employees in the process changes that affect them. Not only is it their right, but also they are the best source of ideas.*

The second principle was, in fact, the answer to a problem we had put off earlier on. When we first met to formulate our vision statement, objectives, and core values, we knew that "teams" would be the instruments to carry them out, but at that time we didn't know exactly how a team would be structured or who would be on it. Now the answer was apparent.

> 2. *The composition of a team is based on the steps required to produce a given product or service. Teams are product and communication based. Here again, the employees themselves are best equipped to identify with whom they need to work and talk to make up any given team.*

Then we paused for a moment to develop a corollary to this principle that would anticipate what some people might consider an exception to the rule.

> 3. *Even in large plants with extensive capital equipment where production processes are spread out over a wide area, teams can still be used and should be assembled in the same way. However, when team members are not actually working together shoulder-to-shoulder, greater emphasis must be placed on joining them together with appropriate communication techniques than on the physical layout of the production line.*

Finally, we finished up with one last principle that we called "Internal Customer Focus."

4. *Production processes work best if all the people involved think of each other as customers and offer each other the same high standards of quality workmanship and service that they would give to customers outside the company.*

The entire plant felt good about the work that had been done on process change. But in the weeks ahead, as the Unmanagers coordinated all the details required to actually put the modules in place, they discovered that even as they conquered one summit, another one presented itself. It would not be enough to simply rearrange people and work areas into new combinations. Under the new format, each of the modules was beginning to look more and more like a small, independent business. Individual team members were, in effect, becoming partners in an entrepreneurial activity, and if they were to succeed, they would obviously have to learn a wide variety of new skills that they had never been expected to use before. And this is where we directed our attention next — training the entire workforce.

Although many people were frightened by the prospect of taking on new roles on the teams, they calmed down when they realized that if weird Dave Polanski could do it, more than likely they could, too. Already a new corporate culture was growing within FineFax, replete with its own folklore that had begun to celebrate the great adventure into the uncharted territory of Unmanagement, and Dave Polanski was one of its heroes. For his insights and willingness to show true affection for his colleagues, Dave was officially recognized as a "Hero of Unmanagement" and was christened "Ergonomic Dave," a bona fide "people person."

I have to tell you, though, this "new" Dave was a mixed blessing for a while. Although he no longer fretted over his image, it was more difficult for him to give up his tendency to overreact. Utterly thrilled by his new status as a "people person," Dave took to reading books by Dr. Leo Buscaglia, the noted author and public speaker known to his many fans as "The Love Doctor." After that, we all had to endure a week or two during which Dave insisted on hugging the person closest to him before getting down to business.

Chapter Thirteen

TRISHA AND THE LION TAMER

It was a cold winter's morning, a few hours before I was to leave home for work, when I woke up in a sweat. I'd had a dream that left me shaking under my layers of blankets. My husband, who was a light sleeper, noticed I was sitting up.

"What is it?," he asked.

"I'm scared," I told him. "I just dreamed I was standing in front of a lion's cage and Treddle was inside, holding a whip and chair, but there was no lion."

"I guess that means the whip was meant for you," he suggested, not too helpfully.

"Yeah, well, I'm supposed to meet with him today because my 60 days are almost up, and I'm afraid I don't have much to show him." It was true. Sure, we had tried to institute some cosmetic changes in the company, improving the physical environment and adjusting the dress code. And we had worked on making managers a little less commanding and a little more facilitating. We also made a few adjustments to the production line that probably, in the long run, would save us money and time. But I didn't have any hard-core evidence of how these changes would affect bottom-line business objectives, and I knew I'd need a lot more time before there would be any marked improvements.

"What would an Unmanager in your situation do?," my husband asked me.

"She would discuss it with the rest of her team," I replied automatically. "But I don't know that this particular situation really lends itself to Unmanagement principles."

"Why not?" he asked.

Why not, I thought. Maybe he had a point. The next time I opened my eyes, the alarm clock was playing symphonic music. It was 6 a.m. and time to get ready for work. I got to the office earlier than usual and started calling around to a few of my trusted Unmanagers. My meeting with Treddle was set for 11 a.m., so I didn't have much time.

A half hour later, with everyone in my office, I laid out the situation. "If you have any desire to see Unmanagement succeed, you've got to help me convince Treddle that it's worthwhile to continue making changes to the plant."

"What would convince him?" Ergonomic Dave asked.

"He asked to see improvements that would help us meet our business objectives, the ones I mentioned in my Kansas speech," I responded.

"Well, that's crazy," Jack Johnson practically shouted. "We haven't had nearly enough time." I agreed that two months' time wasn't enough for any sensible business management program to be implemented.

"We can think of something," someone else said. A few more people agreed.

As fate would have it, at that exact moment my phone rang. Reflecting on the situation now, I can only assume that someone was looking out for my best interests, or perhaps the best interests of the company. At the time, I only remember thinking I had rotten luck.

It was someone from the production department. That person asked to speak to Dave Ballard, and as soon as he picked up the receiver, I saw his whole body visibly shrink.

"They said what?" he asked. "How many?" his voice was a little lower when he asked this question. "Yup," was the last thing he said, before he placed the receiver down. Then he walked slowly back to where he was sitting, his face almost touching the floor as he walked.

We were all a little concerned, and it took Dave a few minutes before he could tell us what was going on. To make a long story short, a major customer had just canceled a huge order. It seems the customer thought his company had okayed the order, but his proposal was ultimately rejected and he had to cancel with us. Even though we had instituted our Just-in-Time inventory system, things were still a mess. We now had all this inventory sitting in the plant, unsold.

I told everybody to take a short break, assess the damage within their own departments, and meet back in my office in 30 minutes. I made it clear that I wanted a representative from every department within the plant to attend the meeting. If Unmanagement were ever put to the test, it would be now. It wasn't too long after everyone cleared out that the phone rang again. Not surprisingly, it was Walter Treddle. He had already received the bad news and was wondering what I was planning to do about it.

I told him that I had already had things under control, that my people were working on the situation, and that I would get back to him in the next few hours. Thankfully, he postponed our 11:00 meeting and said to keep him posted.

Reshuffling the Deck

When my Unmanagement team returned, we all put our heads together and brainstormed. Several good ideas came out of this meeting, although most of them weren't viable. Someone asked if we could find a distributor to take the inventory off our hands at the last minute. Someone else suggested we might look into the costs of warehousing, although that suggestion was struck down pretty quickly as being too expensive. Someone else suggested we offer the equipment at a special sale rate, although that still wouldn't guarantee we could move it fast enough. Finally, someone from Customer Service suggested we might try to patch things up with the customer and that was when a lightbulb went off for the customer service facilitator, Joanne Martin.

"Oh, my gosh," she exclaimed. Joanne had a high-pitched voice and a sweet demeanor. Her personality was often compared to that of the movie actress Melanie Griffith, although physically, she probably was closer to Marion Ross, the mom from the old television show *Happy Days*. Anyway, her squeal of amazement so startled everyone that they burst out in laughter. Then, of course, Joanne turned beet red and it took a few moments before we could quiet down the room again and get Joanne to tell us what she discovered.

"I just realized I had another customer order that we had to delay," she said. "In fact, this is the perfect solution," she exclaimed again, her voice going up a half-octave in her excitement. "You see, Ralph Albertson of Albertson's Merchandise Centers needed 500 units of our Model 4M Fax next week for a big opening he's having. I told him that we normally needed three weeks to build the product. He seemed disappointed that he couldn't have them for the opening, but then he blamed himself for waiting so long to call."

At this point, Dave Polanski interrupted. "I get it. You're saying if we reconfigure the model 384s that we're stuck with now, with just a little cost, we could convert them into 4Ms and meet Albertson's due date."

"I think materials could handle it," chimed in Jack Johnson.

"Production wouldn't be a problem," Dave Ballard confirmed.

"And we'd have one very happy customer," Joanne announced and looked around the room proudly. I could have hugged her. It was perfect.

From the back of the room, I heard someone clear his throat and then, as people shifted around, Walter Treddle appeared from the crowd. I was a little startled to see him because usually he called before he came over to the plant.

"That's an interesting solution," he said, "but I certainly hope you can execute it as easily as you've discussed it. Otherwise, it will be a total fiasco that will embarrass this company."

Everyone stood around, struck silent by his menacing words. Finally, one of the accounting people suggested we all head back to our offices, and I seconded the motion.

The next few days were a blur as everyone worked double duty to fulfill the modified order. I was proud of everyone's commitment to resolving what could have been a devastating problem, not only to our plant, but also to the whole concept of Unmanagement. It was a great relief to know, only after a few days, that the new order had gone out to Albertson's right on schedule.

A week later, customer service called to tell me that Ralph Albertson had been very pleased with our service and had mentioned our company and what a fine job we had done in a local newspaper article about his new store.

A Last-Minute Reprieve

By that time, I had already met with Walter Treddle to give him the good news. And no, he wasn't holding a whip. Actually, things went a lot better than I had originally anticipated. Our hard work bought us an extension of several more months, although he wouldn't give me a specific time frame. Instead, he assured me that he would continue to monitor the plant carefully to make sure this new management approach was working smoothly. I had no doubt in my mind that he would. But I wasn't worried about him, and I found myself falling asleep that night as soon as my head hit the pillow. In fact, after that meeting, I continued to sleep through the night without any more bad dreams. This was a good thing, too, because I needed my rest if I was going to take our Unmanagement process to the next step. It was bound to use up all my energy, and then some.

Chapter Fourteen

FEELS LIKE TEAM SPIRIT

P umped up by our great success with Albertson's fax order and with changing process on the production line, the FineFax Unmanagers now charged off in all directions to educate the entire workforce. Ours was a noble cause; we were dedicated; we were resolute; we were indefatigable.

Then we hit a little snag. Now that we had come to the "people" area on our list of Unmanagement areas that needed improvement, we discovered that in all the excitement we had failed to answer one very interesting question, namely, "What is it exactly that we're supposed to teach people anyway?"

Worse still, it was a question that became more difficult to answer the more we thought about it. For one thing, we could no longer fall back on conventional approaches to the problem. I mean, in most other companies, managers faced with our dilemma would simply have turned to their training department or human resources department, which in turn would have invented some type of curriculum on its own and later unloaded it on an unsuspecting and often unwilling workforce. But FineFax couldn't do that. We were no longer like other companies, and such dictates from on high were not in keeping with the democratic principles of Unmanagement. So, once again, FineFax had to depart from tradition and break new ground.

After some discussion, we decided the first thing we needed to do before we began examining job roles was to reexamine our definition of teams. People knew how to gather informally to create a new unit we called a team, but we needed something better than just informal gatherings. We had to figure out how we could create teams that were successful and productive.

The Team Model

Deciding what skills are needed to create a successful team is a difficult challenge. We had to look at issues that were important in the workplace, both as individuals and collectively. Someone suggested we all make lists of what we should accomplish as a team. Someone else suggested we model our team performance after the criteria we used to measure individual performance. Ironically, we decided the best way to determine what skills a team needs to function effectively was to break up into our own teams and make lists of successful team characteristics. We all brainstormed for a couple hours and eventually narrowed down the list to ten areas we thought teams should focus on. By discussing each of these areas in greater depth, a team could define its own standards and criteria.

It seemed easy enough to create, but something was bothering me about this approach. How could we ensure that the skills we were creating together as teams would be put into practice? How could they be measured? That's when one of the employees suggested we have a handbook, like the kind they use for the Girl Scouts, but ours would be developed during the team training sessions, and it would ensure that the team training was enforced, measurable, and auditable.

Based on that suggestion, we developed the Team Handbook, to be used when conducting the team training sessions. We held our first sessions the following week. These training sessions turned out to be a company-wide affair. Everyone from managers to supervisors to employees came together to learn about the best ways to create a team environment. By the way, this was another terrific opportunity to break down the barriers between management and staff. Having everyone train together meant that we all had to let down our guard and show that no one knew everything. It was a very humbling experience.

The first team training we did focused on Team Building. This was probably the most fundamental training, but without it, we couldn't move forward. Susan, whom we elected our team trainer, started asking questions like "What does change mean?" and "How do teams and team leaders evolve?" and even "Why is this Team Handbook important?" Then everyone reviewed how to apply the team concept to the workplace and what creating teams would mean to the future of FineFax. It was very illuminating to listen to the variety of responses, and it showed me that our company had hired a number of intelligent people who actually cared about the company's future. I think other people noticed, too, because everyone developed a certain camaraderie and respect for each other that day that still continues throughout the plant.

Training sessions number two and three got a little more specific. Known to the accounting folk as the "touchy-feely" sessions, here the focus was on team interpersonal and listening skills. We even managed to come up with a self-improvement personality plan that helped people deal more effectively with team members. Don't worry — we didn't plunge too deeply into issues best left for a professional. This plan focused more on learning basic people skills such as conflict resolution.

I especially enjoyed the sessions on brushing up my listening skills. After taking a listening quiz and failing miserably, I saw that those Truth and Honesty Sessions were truly very effective. I had already made becoming a better listener one of my personal goals, and now I had even more information on how I could improve. I don't mean to brag, but after a while, I started to be so good at listening, I was nicknamed "Spock" after that renowned *Star Trek* hero with the remarkable ears.

Functioning as a Team

The next training session focused on guidelines. We called this "Team Expectations and Rules." Sometimes when you try so hard to be flexible, you end up being disorganized and unfocused. After all, *Unmanagement* didn't have to mean *Unmanageable*. In this session we worked hard to define team expectations of behavior and the rules we needed to make sure our team operated smoothly. I knew that people liked freedom, but in this session I learned they also liked structure.

"Team Brainstorming," session five, was attended with enthusiasm. That's probably because the brainstorming most people were used to involved food and always involved laughter. In the past, our brainstorming sessions were freewheeling, but again we learned the importance of structure. We needed to create a process for reaching a consensus and making effective decisions when timing was critical. We came up with rules for brainstorming that actually cut our meeting time by half! Of course, there would still be plenty of laughter, just not as much time to eat the food. By the way, I heard a few complaints about that later; some people are impossible to please.

I was actually surprised by the topic of the next training session, which was "Team Meetings." With all the changes and improvements we had already made to our meetings, I couldn't imagine a training session on the topic. Yet, I have to admit that after the session, I couldn't believe how much time was wasted in meetings before Unmanagement. We decided to develop a standard meeting agenda that cut down preparation time considerably. We also established how frequently teams should meet and what roles people would play in these meetings. Suddenly our meetings were focused on outcomes and consensus-building. It got so that in those rare moments when a meeting ended without a specific outcome, we felt as if we had failed — although that surely wasn't the case. You can imagine how this improved our overall productivity.

Marcia's Magic Moment

As I sat in my office reviewing what we'd done in the last few weeks, I was very impressed by how well our training sessions had been going. After all, this team approach was a drastic departure from the way things had been structured in the past. It was a brand-new mentality that took a lot of getting used to. And don't think for one minute, people had an easy time adjusting. Anytime you ask people to give up their status, share their authority, and let go of control, it's going to cause a few ripples.

This was most evident to me the day after we had the session on team meetings. One of my supervisors in human resources, of all places, was still having trouble adjusting to Unmanagement. Marcia Knight had been with the company for seven years and was promoted to supervisor fairly recently. While she certainly had enough skills to qualify for the position, I got the impression that she was also promoted because she felt it was her due. The previous supervisor had resigned, and Marcia convinced everyone that she was ready to step into the vacant spot.

Unfortunately, Marcia had not had a lot of management experience and had the wrong ideas about what it meant to be a manager. She bullied her staff, tried to keep people down, and was generally insecure about her role in the department. So, it came as no surprise to me when I walked in on her issuing instructions to her new assistant, Linda Lavey. Linda had only been in her job for a few months and was almost fresh out of college. This would be her first real business experience, and Marcia was not making it a positive one.

"Look, Linda," I heard her saying, "all I want you to do is classify these files according to index number. Don't ask me why, I don't have time to tell you, and even if I did, it's probably not important for you to know. Someday, when you have a job like mine, you'll appreciate all the routine things you're doing now, and it will all fall into place."

From Linda's expression, I could tell she was feeling a bit demeaned and resentful. Unmanagement certainly hadn't found its place in human resources.

"Marcia," I said as I poked my head around the corner, "could I see you in my office, please?"

She was there in a matter of moments.

"Marcia," I began. I realized I had to be careful how I addressed this transgression; I needed to incorporate the principles of Unmanagement myself in doing so.

"You know, Marcia," I began again, "I've been thinking about some of the Unmanagement principles we've been practicing lately, and I think we're making a lot of changes for people to digest all at once, especially the employees."

She nodded with a concerned look on her face. "Oh, yes. I think my staff has had a lot to adjust to in a short period of time."

I could probably say the same for you, I thought. Instead, I agreed. "But I think if some of the employees saw how effectively other employees and managers were handling the changes, they would be inspired to try harder themselves. So, what I'd like to do is make your department the model for other departments to follow. I think if you could work up a few examples that demonstrate how you have put Unmanagement principles to work in your department and share them with the others, that could be very effective."

She nodded again.

"So," I continued. "Tell me, do you have some ideas of what you're going to share with us?"

She stared at me for a second. "We...well... ," she stammered.

"Because, you know, Marcia, I have absolute faith in your ability to become one of the best prototypes for Unmanagement this company has ever seen. And, just as I'm doing with you, for example, by telling you my objectives, giving you a lot of authority and leeway to carry them out and leaving the door open for my input, but only if you need it," I took a deep breath here, "I know that you probably already do the same with your staff. So you probably are very close, anyway, to becoming a wonderful model of Unmanagement."

I smiled and paused again. "And as the very essence of an Unmanager, I'm sure your staff will want to share in their own words some of the ways they've seen you practice these principles as well."

"Absolutely," Marcia said. Her cheeks were a little flushed, and I took it as a sign that, whether or not she would acknowledge it, things were going to be different in the human resources department from now on.

A few days later, as I walked by her office, I overheard Linda talking to a friend on the phone, telling her that she was feeling a little better about her job and that suddenly, her boss had started giving her a lot more responsibility and sharing a lot more information. See, Unmanagement can work wonders, but only if everyone is in on it together.

Getting Down to Business

During our next training session on "Team Decision Making," we actually hit a snag. One of the team members during the session felt it was impossible to make decisions as a team and that we shouldn't even spend time trying to learn how. When our facilitator, Susan, asked for a vote on whether people agreed with this assessment, some other people in the back didn't even bother to raise their hands. It was clear that we had to figure out a process that would take into account everyone's input — indeed, we had to ensure it. I've since discovered that when teams know what to expect, they can get down to business. Having a clear methodology for making decisions guarantees that the whole process flows more smoothly.

Clearly, our training sessions could be classified in one of two ways: how teams will function in and of themselves, and how they will function within the company. Our next training session fell into the second category. "Team Business Focus" asked teams to define their role in meeting the company's overall business objectives. For example, if one of FineFax's objectives was to reduce operating costs, then the team would have to define how it might best work toward that objective. The team would then have to establish and track goals, figure out how to measure its success in meeting those goals, and decide what to do when the goals fell below target. It was a good thing the team had its training in decision making before this session. It took a long time to hammer out a business focus and ways to accomplish it. This was a difficult session and probably one of the most important ones we held.

The final two sessions were back to back. The first, "Team Roles and Responsibilities," asked each member to take on a team role, define what the role entailed, and be prepared to rotate into a new role as the team matured. We refined this training session as we went along, but I'll tell you more about that later. The second session, "Team Recognition," emphasized the importance of acknowledging the accomplishments of both team members and teams as a whole and established methods for communicating those successes to the rest of the company. It was the perfect session to conclude all the training we had done because I had decided that afternoon to hold a small party to reward everyone's participation and willingness to tackle team management.

The entire training process took several weeks. Overall, it was a much more complex process than what I am describing to you here. But just so you can see more clearly what we covered, I've created a list of the sessions for you. In the words of the immortal David Letterman, folks, here is my version of the "Top Ten List."

Trisha's Top Ten List of Team Training Sessions

10. Team Building

9. Team Interpersonal Skills

8. Team Listening Skills

7. Team Expectations and Rules

6. Team Brainstorming

5. Team Meetings

4. Team Decision Making

3. Team Business Focus

2. Team Roles & Responsibilities

1. Team Recognition

Chapter Fifteen

"OPERATION EGGHEAD"

Now that we had organized our teams and taught them the fundamental skills they needed to function, we hit an impasse. While people now had the skills to work well together, they still had no idea of what they were supposed to do.

That was a real headache. Of course, we knew that the teams had to keep doing all those things they'd been doing right along to produce. But, after all, this was Unmanagement, the dawn of a new era in which employees were supposed to take on management responsibilities. Surely we hadn't come all this way just to leave the employees in the same old rut. But what exactly were those new responsibilities?

I got together with my staff, and we stewed over this question for hours, getting nowhere. I reached the point where I was feeling the same kind of frustration and fear that I had felt in my television room when I first came upon the idea of Unmanagement. The whole job just seemed so enormous! How was I ever going to do it all? Fortunately, the realization that saved me back then bailed me out again.

"I think the answer's been right in front of us all along," I said, acting on an inspiration, "but we haven't been able to see it because we're still acting like the managers we used to be, trying to do everything ourselves. All we have to do is follow our own principles of Unmanagement, in this case: *If you want to find out what to teach people, ask them what they need to know.*"

"Well, all that's fine, Trisha," Franklin Dell said, "but it still doesn't tell us what the teams are supposed to do. So the way I look at it, we're right back where we started."

"But, Franklin," I said, "it's really the same question. But you can't just go out and ask someone, 'Hey, what do you need to know?' That's too broad, too loose. There's a better way. We're looking for what a team should do, right? So why don't we go out and ask our future team members which of their supervisors' responsibilities can be taken over by the team. Then, depending on what they say, we'll know what to teach them."

My plan attracted some interest, and soon we all fanned out to survey the plant. Later we sorted through the responses and found that what we had was, in effect, a complete roster of management responsibilities that the employees felt they could take on. I think you might find it particularly interesting because, although it reflects the FineFax manufacturing bias a little bit, for the most part these are responsibilities that could be expected of any team in any business.

The Basic Work of Teamwork

Attendance	Disciplinary Action
Costs	Efficiency
Budgets	Problem Resolution
Training	Product Quality
Communications	Hiring
Product Output	Scrap
Scheduling	Peer Reviews

Now we had something concrete. Using the new roster as a guide, we created a new program of Unmanagement that would teach employees everything they needed to know so that they could take on some of the management responsibilities previously left to the supervisors. We devised a comprehensive, educational program for FineFax that had five parts:

The Parts of a Training Program

1. Orientation and Job Skills

2. Business Knowledge

3. Interpersonal Skills

4. Ethics and Values

5. Job Rotation

We also decided on several underlying principles that would shape how training was delivered:

The Training Code

1. Training is everyone's right and responsibility, and everyone is in training.

2. Ask people what they need to know.

3. Classes can be structured or unstructured. Knowledge is the objective, so use whatever method works.

4. Use other employees as trainers wherever possible.

5. Let employees use what they've learned immediately and then follow up periodically. Immediate application and follow-up are the keys to success.

And so was born the legendary "Operation Egghead."

Nobody at FineFax had ever seen anything quite like it. For two weeks, the entire employee population revolved through a series of seminars and classes designed to prepare them for their new roles on the teams, after which, they were told, they would all be genuine "eggheads" — official know-it-alls. As usual, the actual timing of the classes was designed around the plant's daily production schedule. Most classes were taught during normal working hours, except for a few sessions that spilled over into a Saturday, during which employees were paid time-and-a-half for attending. We hoped to present each subject area in as much detail as possible given the time constraints, but in any event we guaranteed that employees would at least get a good working overview of any subject.

It is important for me to stress here that at no time did we allow the training sessions to interfere with our work at the plant, or Treddle would have been on us in a matter of minutes. Instead, we trained only when the business allowed us to. This also meant that our training sessions were usually short and to the point. It took some time for all the trainers to get the hang of it, but after a while everyone was pretty much involved in everything. The training process required a lot of flexibility — it was an organizational challenge, but one that FineFax was able to meet splendidly.

In my opinion, an event like Operation Egghead is very important to the practice of Unmanagement in any company for several reasons:

Why Egghead Is Important

1. More than any other single event, it actually announces the launch of Unmanagement. For the first time, the various components of Unmanagement are gathered together and presented as a single comprehensive and cohesive program to the entire employee population.

2. It recognizes the importance of training everyone at the same time so they will all be pulling in the same direction.

3. It is an extremely effective and exciting "visual commitment to change."

Since there are bound to be individual differences from company to company, I've decided that it would probably work out best if I just described what we actually did at FineFax, and then you can pick and choose what you like. Let's start from the beginning.

Orientation and Job Skills

During Operation Egghead we avoided teaching job skills per se, because that involved a high degree of individual attention unsuited to the broad group coverage Egghead had been designed to achieve. We did describe in some detail, however, how job skills would be taught in the future, changing what for us had been a relatively haphazard affair into one that was more carefully structured and thought out. There were five components to the orientation and job skills section of our training program.

1. General Orientation. In the future, we said, employees would actually begin acquiring the skills they needed to work at FineFax at an orientation session before they took their place on the production line. There were certain ideas and concepts which, although they had nothing to do with soldering a circuit board, were nonetheless essential to the employees' success at FineFax. In a sense, the orientation would be much like a mini-Operation Egghead because, when a new employee sits down for orientation, that employee gets:

- an overview of FineFax products and services;

- an overview of FineFax vision, mission, objectives, and values;

- an overview of FineFax's business results and position in the marketplace;

- a list of resource people.

Of course, your company may already be giving orientation sessions to newly hired employees, but what I'm proposing here is a bit different. There will certainly be a greater emphasis on business results. But that isn't the largest difference because, you see, the members of the teams are going to give the orientation sessions themselves instead of, say, your human resources department. And it's important that they do that because they're also going to be responsible for another little shocker, which is that team members will also be doing their own hiring. Later on I'll discuss more about how that happens.

2. Specific Skills Training. Immediately after a new employee has gone through orientation, we intend to give the employee hands-on training in the specific job the employee was hired to perform. At this point, he or she should be trained by a team member and by the team's facilitator.

3. Assessment/Certification. Next, the employee's progress in mastering the skills required would be assessed and the employee would be "certified" to begin work.

4. Buddy System. Then the employee gets more on-the-job training by working side-by-side for a short period of time with another team member in a "buddy-system" arrangement to ensure that the new employee blends smoothly into team life.

5. Annual Recertification. Finally, all employees would be asked to get recertified once each year as a way of demonstrating that their skills are being maintained at high levels.

Business Knowledge

One of the most important discoveries I made early on during my conversations and interviews with employees was that, except for bits and pieces they had picked up on their own, their overall understanding of business principles and business terminology was very limited. If you want to get a sense of how much your own employees know, try using this surprisingly revealing exercise I worked up.

My own results with the exercise had come in at the "ugly" level, so don't feel bad if your scores are disappointing. On the positive side, though, I can say that I also found that employees were not lacking for interest in the subject. Actually, most employees wanted to know more about business. But over the years, it had been drummed into their heads that this kind of information was the exclusive province of management. In general, management had concluded that it was unnecessary to share information about FineFax's business results with employees because they had mistakenly assumed that the employees couldn't understand it and weren't interested anyway. When Unmanagement comes on the scene, this dinosaur of an atti-

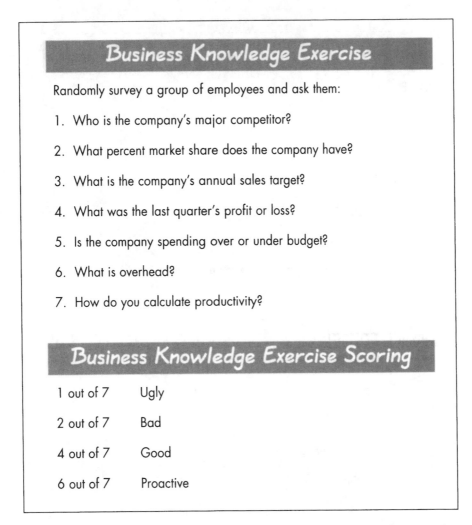

Business Knowledge Exercise

Randomly survey a group of employees and ask them:

1. Who is the company's major competitor?

2. What percent market share does the company have?

3. What is the company's annual sales target?

4. What was the last quarter's profit or loss?

5. Is the company spending over or under budget?

6. What is overhead?

7. How do you calculate productivity?

Business Knowledge Exercise Scoring

1 out of 7	Ugly
2 out of 7	Bad
4 out of 7	Good
6 out of 7	Proactive

tude is destined for extinction because, not only does it demean the employees' intelligence, but also it looms large as a barrier between managers and employees.

With Operation Egghead, we brought the resources of the entire organization to bear on the problem. First we developed a list of subjects we wanted to cover:

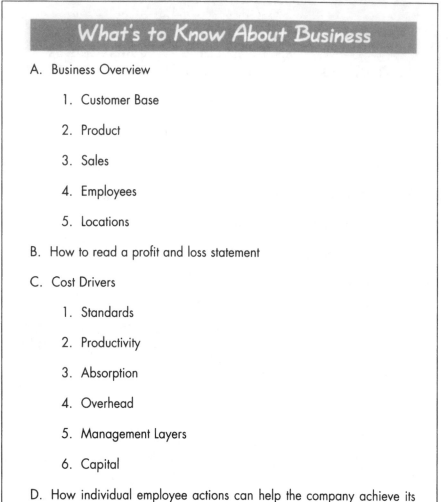

What's to Know About Business

A. Business Overview

    1. Customer Base

    2. Product

    3. Sales

    4. Employees

    5. Locations

B. How to read a profit and loss statement

C. Cost Drivers

    1. Standards

    2. Productivity

    3. Absorption

    4. Overhead

    5. Management Layers

    6. Capital

D. How individual employee actions can help the company achieve its business objectives

Then we got various departments within FineFax to actually teach the courses. Although we had nothing against bringing in trainers from outside the company to teach employees, it wasn't necessary in this case because we already had sufficient expertise in-house. For example, the FineFax marketing people went over the company's products and markets; the accounting department reviewed the profit and loss statement; engineering discussed manufacturing efficiency, and so on. The courses were seldom dull because the instructors, unused to their new roles, resorted to various improvisations as they went along, which often turned out to be hilarious — Mr. Potato Head being an excellent case in point.

Mr. Potato Head Teaches School

The Unmanagers hoped to make training entertaining as well as informative, and often that produced some novel developments. In one memorable case, the engineering department came up with a decidedly unique way to explain what a "standard" is. The engineers wanted to show that each of FineFax's products should at least be made in a "standard" amount of time, so they had employees assemble a child's game called "Mr. Potato Head" as an example.

Mr. Potato Head is a plastic model meant to resemble a potato onto which kids can stick small plastic ears, eyes, nose, and mouth to produce a fanciful and amusing cartoonlike character. Each time the employees assembled Mr. Potato Head, they found they got faster at the job and reached an efficient and fluid pace that was neither too fast nor too slow. And that, the engineers explained, was the "standard" assembly time for Mr. Potato Head.

Standards were especially important to a manufacturing business, the engineers explained, because it helped them forecast how much product any given production line could turn out in a given period of time, as well as the cost of direct labor involved in that production process. The engineers explained that, although they used more precise techniques called "time and motion studies" to get at the standard, the basic principles were still the same.

After every presentation, we passed out handouts that everybody could use later on to review what they had learned.

Interpersonal Skills

In the new team training, we had already started to get our people used to the importance of interpersonal skills. If you'll remember, it was one of our 10 principles. The difference between the interpersonal skills used within teams vs. the interpersonal skills taught here was that here, teams were getting a more specific approach to the policies and principles that management, in the past, had reserved solely for itself

Let's go through them one at a time so I can give you a better idea of what we did.

Race Relations. At FineFax, the workforce was very diverse. Although relations had been good, FineFax was still much like society at large where narrow-minded attitudes are often founded on random, irrational prejudices. To announce our commitment to absolute equality, we brought in a trained facilitator from outside the plant to help employees examine and improve their understanding of cultural differences. This particular feature of the interpersonal curriculum was designed to begin with a general, plant-wide meeting and then to proceed over time with additional sessions in which employees could get together in smaller groups better suited to the emotional intensity that often surrounded the subject.

Negotiating, Listening, and Problem Solving. Here again, employees were taught that being a team member meant compromise and cooperation. No single member would be allowed to dictate the behavior of his or her peers. Instead, team members learned how to listen effectively as others described their assessment of a given problem; then they were trained to use a problem-solving model to methodically separate key points from less relevant considerations. Finally, they learned how to focus on the problem itself, rather than on the personalities involved, so they could negotiate a solution among themselves.

Presentation Skills. In the future, we knew employees were certain to encounter situations in which they might want to change their work environment in some major way — for example, flex hours or plant-sponsored day care for employees' children — that would require the cooperation of senior managers. We decided that in these instances, employees should be expected to make a presentation to senior managers. Furthermore, the presentation should be similar in form, content, and quality to the type of presentation any of the senior managers would have to make themselves if they wanted to change something in the business. Then we taught them how to put such a presentation together.

Situational Leadership. To give team members more confidence and to inspire them to participate more energetically in the life of the team, we relied on a series of reenactments of actual events. For example, two employees had gotten into a heated argument because one thought the other's way of working was slowing down the production line. Eventually, a supervisor had to break it up. Operation Egghead used situations like this

The Five Parts of an Effective Business Proposal

1. Define the change and its scope.

2. Identify the benefits and risks of the change.

3. Identify what specific business indices it will affect.

4. Quantify how much it will cost to make the change.

5. Identify how long it will take to evaluate the change before a "go" or "no-go" decision is made and identify what measurements will be used to make the evaluation.

as teaching tools. The employees involved were first asked for permission, and then the argument was reenacted for a larger group of employees. The group members were then asked to compare how they would have handled the argument with the supervisor's actual response.

Hiring. From time to time, FineFax would be overwhelmed with a sudden influx of orders. To meet the workload, the personnel department hired temporary employees. This response had its good and bad points. Although the work invariably got done, often the temporary employees didn't fit in well with the employees already on the production line. Bickering and squabbling on the line often made the whole experience more painful than productive. For a long time, no one had a better solution. Then, one day an unusually large order appeared. The need for temporary employees was so great that the personnel people simply weren't able to interview all the temporary help by themselves. As a result, existing employees were asked to do some of the interviewing. Although personnel had been terrified that this emergency measure would produce absolute chaos, it turned out that the people selected by the employees actually worked out much better than others had in the past. There were fewer disagreements, and the production process moved along more smoothly. In several instances, the temporary employees turned out to be so good that they were later invited back to join FineFax permanently. This experience finally made us realize that even though the idea was extremely unconventional, it nonetheless made great sense that employees should be allowed to hire the people with whom they were going to work. After all, who knew better what kind of person it took to get a particular job done than the employees themselves?

But making employee hiring one of FineFax's official corporate policies required thoughtful preparation. And Operation Egghead was a large part of that preparation because, again using the situational leadership approach, we showed employees how to conduct interviews properly and made them aware of some questions that could not be asked of potential employees because they were against the law.

Play. Although some of the learning activities involved in interpersonal training were also team-building activities, such as group problem solving and situational leadership, we also realized that team spirit welled up from team members playing together just as much as it did from their working together. To make sure that FineFax understood that play was henceforth an officially sanctioned event, we announced that at the end of Operation Egghead there would be a "lip sync" contest open to all employees who were wacky enough to enter. Furthermore, we said the contest was only the first of many future activities that would include softball and volleyball tournaments, a fashion show, a carnival, cookouts, and charitable fund-raising drives in the local community.

You can imagine the kind of positive feedback we received for this announcement. People had already started to plan what they would do together for the contest during breaks and lunch periods. There were many multitalented people at the plant who never had the opportunity to show off their hidden abilities. People formed new bonds with each other and learned things about one another that they may have otherwise never discovered. And it only served to make the teams stronger than ever.

All in all, the training sessions had been going very well. We had gotten through the first three parts nearly unscathed. Unfortunately, things don't always go as planned, and it was right before we were about to teach one of the most crucial sections of the training program that everything we had stressed up to that point took an unexpected turn.

Chapter Sixteen

TROUBLE IN PARADISE

U p to this point, Operation Egghead had been moving along smoothly. In every way, the program seemed to be achieving its goal of helping people get along with one another and work together more effectively. But there now occurred a surprising and instructive incident that had exactly the opposite effect. Rather than harmony, fighting broke out in the ranks, and the entire program came to an abrupt and alarming halt.

I was on my way to the shipping dock to check on delivery schedules when I first learned that conditions in the plant were other than I'd hoped. As I passed by the production line, I suddenly heard a man and a woman yelling at each other. And when I turned toward the sound, I saw Alice Muncie and Victor Salazar squared off against each other inside a tight circle of onlookers that was expanding quickly as other employees left their positions on the line.

"Look, Victor," Alice shouted, "since when do you decide what we should be doing?"

"Wake up, Alice," Victor yelled back, "we're supposed to be doing it. I just learned about it, so trust me. You want to lose your job?" Then the crowd started offering free advice, which raised the decibel level of the whole confrontation even higher.

I plowed through the crowd hollering, "Wait a minute! Wait a minute! Time out!" I got between Alice and Victor and tried to find out what was going on, but everyone was too agitated to make much sense out of the argument. So I asked everybody to get back to work while I talked with the two opponents in my office.

During that interview, the cause of the disagreement surfaced quickly. The logistics of training everyone in the plant, while at the same time keeping enough people on the line to get the work out, inevitably meant that at times some employees were working with other employees who had yet to attend the same class the first group had just completed. In planning Operation Egghead, we had foreseen the unavoidable overlap in the scheduling, but we had not, and really couldn't have, anticipated its consequences. The problem was that the first group of employees wanted to use some of the techniques they had learned immediately, and the other employees, who had yet to be similarly trained, resented this pressure from their peers. Victor, for example, had tried a bit too forcefully to get Alice involved in a new technique he had just learned. She had resisted because she had yet to complete all the training that he had.

Concerned that Unmanagement was about to unravel before it had a chance to get going, I canceled the training classes for that day and immediately scheduled meetings with each of the plant's three shifts. At the meetings, I outlined what had happened between Alice and Victor and said that although I regretted the unfortunate incident, it had taught me another important principle about Unmanagement: *No one should try any of the new Unmanagement techniques until everyone in the plant has completed the training program.*

Then I finished up by saying, "I know many of you people have some great ideas you want to try out, but please hold on to them just a little longer until we can all work on them together."

This incident is worth remembering. It certainly caught me by surprise, and I can only think that, if you're prepared for it, you're way ahead of the game.

Ethics and Values

The next day, Operation Egghead started up again with classes on ethics and values, the fourth part of the training program. You could feel tension in the air because no one was sure whether Egghead could recover gracefully from its setback the day before. But Egghead got a break. Exactly when it needed one the most, FineFax discovered its second "Hero of Unmanagement."

We'd made ethics and values part of Egghead because we wanted to make sure everyone understood that how employees treated each other was just as important as the quantity of their output, that there were "hard" values and objectives measured in numbers and "soft" values and objectives measured in common decency and mutual respect.

Even though I was asked to teach a large part of the sessions on ethics and values because I was the leader of the plant, we also hoped to have an employee do some of the training. At first we didn't know who might be able to fill the role. But after I'd heard about the following incident, the answer was obvious — Ferlin Paige.

Ferlin's involvement in this incident the day before showed me he truly cared about the welfare of his fellow workers. He had been in the cafeteria line, and two people were in front of him, repeating an offensive racial joke that made Ferlin's skin crawl. He couldn't stand the way they were laughing about it, and he spoke up. He told them to stop laughing immediately, explained that the joke didn't demonstrate basic human respect, and asked for their names. Then he made it a point of bringing up the incident at our meeting.

It was interesting to hear various people talk about what they would have done in that situation. Since federal law required us to handle this situation appropriately, we needed to have one consistent approach. We discussed how it was impossible to change people's personal baggage, but it was important to uphold consistent values at the facility. We then came up with a policy and posted it everywhere throughout the plant. Typically, companies post their values on the wall, but they don't necessarily do anything to reinforce them. By holding open discussions on a regular basis, we hoped to demonstrate that we took these issues seriously.

When it was time for Ferlin to take over the meeting, he did a wonderful job. There were other examples of ethics and values that we discussed over time — issues such as whether or not the maintenance people could have pictures of scantily clad women in the changing rooms, or whether our latest advertising brochure had represented a properly diverse group of people in its cover photograph.

In addition, Ferlin told a spellbinding story about the interrelationships among core values, objectives, and vision. And with that, we officially recognized him as our second Hero of Unmanagement.

Job Rotation

During the original development of Operation Egghead, we had reached a point at which, although we had planned for all four of the training sections I just talked about, we still weren't satisfied. Several people had insisted back then that there had to be a way to broaden the training program even more. They wanted to find some method that would show employees that training was an ongoing activity and also give them a way to increase their skills beyond their current job assignments. In short, they wanted employees to keep learning, developing, and growing long after Operation Egghead had ended.

They eventually came up with "Job Rotation," a solution that I thought was inspired. Not only did it accomplish both of the objectives we hoped for, but it also brought into play an especially effective educational principle — there is no better way to learn something than by actually doing it.

The employees learned about Job Rotation for the first time when it was unveiled as a kind of grand finale to Operation Egghead. It could start immediately, they were told, and any area or department in the plant could participate. Here were the rules:

The Rules of Job Rotation

1. Identify and describe the job and any experience requirements.

2. State how long the job is expected to last.

3. Post the job opportunity openly for the entire employee population.

4. Allow the team to interview and choose the appropriate applicant.

5. There will be no change in salary.

6. An employee's original job will not be backfilled while that employee is on job rotation.

7. No job rotation position can last for longer than six months.

8. In any given year, there should be no more than eight job rotation openings to minimize the disruption to schedules that too much job switching might cause.

9. When employees return to their original teams, they must give a full review to their team members of what they learned while they were away.

For example, MIS was behind one quarter and wasn't getting enough done. They posted a notice that they needed someone to fill in for a couple weeks. Jennifer, in production, applied for the position and was chosen to fill in. She had already been taking programming classes at night, so it was an opportunity for her to put her skills to the test. While she was gone, others in the production department had to adjust to her vacancy. When she came back to production, she gave a full report on her responsibilities and what she had learned while working in a new department.

The Cost of Doing Business

Well, that's my cook's tour through the incredible goings-on that was Operation Egghead. But before I move on to tell you about how our new teams handled a crisis, I want to answer a question that has probably been on your mind all along: How much does this cost? From the start, cost was a major concern for us as well — not only the cost of Egghead itself, but also the cost of ongoing training. I was also more than a little curious to see if other companies that might want to try Unmanagement could realistically afford both Egghead and any follow-up courses.

The way I see it, any company that wants to start an Unmanagement training program will have two basic cost variables to deal with: (1) the off-standard cost of the time employees spend in class and not on direct labor making product, and (2) actual cash outlays. Given our estimation of what it takes to get all existing employees fully comfortable with Unmanagement, I think you should be prepared to accommodate an increase in off-standard costs to include about 40 hours of formal classroom training per year for a two-year period. You might cut back on one course or another to reduce the off-standard cost, but I don't think it's wise to go below the 40 hours — which, now that I think about it, should really be looked at as more of a fixed cost than a variable cost.

Although you should leave off-standard time costs alone, you'll have considerably more leeway when it comes to spending cash money. You can control the dollar size of your training budget according to how much of your training uses "homemade," in-house expertise vs. training bought retail from outside your company. The actual mix could vary widely from company to company. Our own experience has shown that most of the training can be done, and done well, in-house; nevertheless, there are times when it makes good sense to bring in outside help, as we did to teach race relations. Obviously, the greater the reliance on outside training, the larger the training budget. In most companies, however, training budgets of some kind already exist, and you'll simply have to reallocate the money to courses tailored specifically for Unmanagement.

Now, here's an important little tip we learned about later on.

Even if your company has little or no money budgeted for training, you can still find ways to underwrite a training program.

How to Self-Finance Training

Training can be a give and take between a company and its employees. For example, once the FineFax employees wanted a particular type of cultural diversity training but, when they checked it out, they discovered that it would cost $100,000 to put everybody through the course. A figure that size was definitely not within the budget. But rather than give up on the course entirely, the Unmanagers and the employees came up with an innovative solution. The employees agreed to self-finance their own education by achieving a 5 percent increase in production efficiency, which could then be used to offset the cost of the course.

I thought Operation Egghead turned out great, and the prospects for continuing education looked good, too. I felt both managers and employees were well on their way to making the transition from the traditional roles they had occupied in the past to their new Unmanagement roles of the future. Ferlin even drew up a chart to illustrate the transition. He called it "People Power."

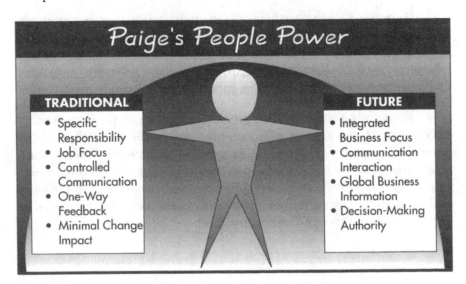

Paige's People Power

TRADITIONAL
- Specific Responsibility
- Job Focus
- Controlled Communication
- One-Way Feedback
- Minimal Change Impact

FUTURE
- Integrated Business Focus
- Communication Interaction
- Global Business Information
- Decision-Making Authority

The Incredible Lip Sync Contest

One week after Operation Egghead ended, on a warm and sunny Saturday afternoon, the long-awaited lip sync contest (if you'll remember, our "officially sanctioned play") finally got under way. In a large, grassy field behind the FineFax plant, employees and their families spread out blankets and began unpacking sandwiches and drinks from coolers. From time to time, they looked up from their snacks to a small, low stage that had been built against the brick wall of the plant. There were several standing microphones on the stage and two loudspeakers. Gradually, as if sensing the show was about to begin, the crowd moved in closer. Then they noticed a long, white Cadillac limousine with darkened glass windows slowly approaching the stage area. The Cadillac stopped and the chauffeur opened its doors to let out four men, who were elegantly attired in evening clothes. They were immediately recognized as four members of the circuit board installation team, and the crowd roared its approval. Acting as if they were used to this kind of attention, as any self-respecting rock stars should be, the four men took their places on stage. They introduced themselves as the "Live Wires" and immediately broke into a frantic rendition of Billy Ocean's song "Get into My Car." As they lip synched the song, the Live Wires also tried to execute a number of fancy dance steps. However, doing both at the same time frequently proved too much for them. More times than not the fancy steps became missteps and then outright stumbles, and the audience members laughed themselves to tears.

Many more acts followed that day, including a trio of women from the accounting department who jumped around on stage in ballet costumes with brightly colored balloons around their waists. And another group, whom no one can adequately describe to this day, lip synched a Golden Oldie while wearing bright red wigs, sport coats, and bathing trunks.

Yours truly also entered the contest. I wore long white gloves and an unbelievably tasteless, powder blue evening gown adorned with maybe 20 pounds of sequins and spangles. I lip synched Madonna's "Material Girl" and carried on shamelessly. However, because I was also wearing outrageous high heels, there were several times when I nearly fell off the stage, only to be righted at the last minute by the closest person in the audience. Other than that, I thought I was pretty good.

Chapter Seventeen

THE FIRST BIG PAYOFF

N ow that everyone had been educated, the time had come to actually create the new teams. We jumped right in, but we would've been better off to take our time because our first attempt didn't work out so well.

We organized the 200 people working in production at FineFax into three teams of between 20 and 25 people on each of the plant's three shifts. The composition of each team followed the new production arrangement that had broken up the single production line into three separate "modules": assemblers, testers, and supervisor. It looked pretty good. From the very start, the teams showed impressive esprit de corps, taking on distinctive names to distinguish themselves from one another. Third-shift teams used names like "Nighthawks" and "All-Nighters," while teams on the first shift chose names such as "Early Risers" and the "Daybreak" team.

Because all the team members were now genuine, certified "eggheads," we simply assumed they were qualified to take on many of the responsibilities they had identified that were previously handled by the plant supervisors. What's more, we thought we should leave them alone to choose the responsibilities they wanted to try first, as well as how they wanted to do them.

This was a big mistake. It was too much to expect of newly formed teams. They quickly got overwhelmed and then generally bogged down in arguing and bad morale. So we all had to back up a bit and reconsider our approach. We realized that we needed to reexamine the team roles and responsibilities we had been teaching in the general team training sessions. Before, we had defined these roles too loosely, allowing each team member to identify his or her function during the course of a meeting. Evidently, we had to be more specific and define team roles that would more closely mirror the responsibilities we used to carry out our business objectives.

After a while, we found an improvement that solved our problem, a process that can also save you a lot of trouble. Basically, you just have to remember that before a team can take on its new responsibilities in full, it must first build an "internal team structure." Here's what we did:

How to Create Internal Team Structure

1. Define responsibilities.

2. Categorize responsibilities into similar functions.

3. Give each category a position and title.

4. Ask team members to volunteer to fill each position.

5. Rotate positions among team members for varying lengths of time, depending on the complexity of the assignment, to maximize knowledge and experience.

6. Every team member must take one of the positions at least once.

The Internal Team Structure at FineFax

Armed with this insight, the FineFax teams started up again. This time they first distributed their particular responsibilities among five positions, and this time they were successful. They came up with the following positions:

1. **Communicator.** The communicator represents the team at all staff and department meetings and reports back to the team. The communicator organizes the team's communication center, posting minutes of meetings, department and management memos, and other items of interest to the team. The communicator is also the liaison between the team and the other teams in the plant.

2. **Materials Focal.** The materials "focal," so-called to highlight the focus of his or her responsibility, keeps track of the priorities of the production schedule: Does the team have any emergencies to contend with? What products have to be completed before others? The materials focal also works with the plant's materials department to make sure that team members have the right raw materials and tools to do their jobs.

3. **Indices Manager.** The indices manager tracks the team's productivity and efficiency, including daily output compared to goals, manufacturing cycle times, and housekeeping and safety statistics. The indices manager charts the statistics and posts them in the communication center.

4. **Quality Focal.** The quality focal measures the quality of the team's output and works closely with the quality auditors in the plant's quality control department. If quality problems should arise, the quality focal must work with the team and any other department to identify the necessary adjustments.

5. **Budget Focal.** The budget focal gathers the statistics that will eventually be used to calculate the plant's overall budget, as well as the team's specific portion of that budget. Those statistics include items such as volume forecasts, tool expense, and training requirements.

Over the next couple weeks, the teams continued to make minor adjustments as they used the new structure, but overall the teams worked extremely well. Still, you could tell that people weren't ready to jump up and down quite yet. Many of the FineFax people realized that the recent work flow had been fairly routine, and they were wondering how the new team structure would hold up when things got tough. They got their answer sooner than they expected early one morning when a crisis struck. I have pieced the story together for you.

Anatomy of a Crisis

7 a.m.: The third shift is just changing over to the first shift. As usual, the communicator from the Nighthawks team on the third shift stays behind to update the entire Daybreak team on the first shift that is taking over the work in the same production module. They had a pretty good night, the Nighthawks communicator says, but there are two late-breaking developments that bear watching. Toward the end of the third shift, the Nighthawks received an emergency order for a customer. This order required that a shipment of certain circuit boards leave the production module within the next six hours. The Nighthawks team had only been able to start in on the order, so the Daybreak team will have to make sure that this emergency turn-around is completed on time. Ordinarily, the assignment wouldn't present much of a problem, but this time there may be a complication. The Nighthawks team communicator explains that late in the shift, the team noticed some "fluctuations" in the functional test yields on some of the other circuit boards they had been working on. In fact, it looked like yields had dropped by about 60 percent, but the event had happened late in the shift and only on a few boards. Therefore, the Nighthawks team still wasn't sure how serious the problem was. Nor could the team say whether a similar problem would show up on the circuit boards in the emergency order. Visual quality inspections had, of course, been made when the defective boards first turned up, but there did not appear to be any soldering problems or wrong parts on the boards involved.

7:10 a.m.: The materials focal for the Daybreak team is meeting with the team. The materials focal reports that the normal workload for the team is down by about 10 percent, which means that the team has two employees who can work for a while on some other team whose workload has increased.

7:20 a.m.: The Daybreak team communicator is meeting with the communicators on the other first-shift teams to go over production and manpower requirements.

7:30 a.m.: The Daybreak team communicator meets with the Daybreak team members and tells them that, yes, one of the other teams can use two more employees to help out. Two Daybreak team members volunteer and leave for their temporary assignment. Work begins on the Daybreak team.

8:30 a.m.: Functional test yields are getting worse, and circuit boards are backing up in front of the test equipment. All told, the Daybreak team is working on five circuit board types, of which three seem to fail the yield tests. So the team decides to shut down the line on those three boards while continuing work on the remaining two. Another Daybreak team member is now available to work on another team, and one volunteers to join the other team members who left earlier.

8:35 a.m.: The Daybreak team materials focal calls in the test engineers, who arrive and begin to study the failure codes produced by the software in the test sets. They quickly determine that the problem is not being caused by any bug in the software.

8:50 a.m.: The Daybreak team quality focal alerts the quality auditors in the quality control department.

9:00 a.m.: Bad news. The materials focal calls the materials department to let it know that the Daybreak team, working with engineering, has just learned that some of the circuit boards failing the functional yield tests are also the same types of boards involved in the emergency turnaround order. As a result, the order may not be completed within the deadline.

9:05 a.m.: The team members call in their facilitator to let him know what they've done so far and to ask if he has any additional suggestions. At this point an incident occurs to mar an otherwise remarkable performance by the team. And it isn't caused by the facilitator.

Instead, it's brought on by Dave Ballard, the plant's overall production manager. The facilitator applauds the team's initiative, but Ballard, who's heard about what was going on, nearly has a nervous breakdown. He thinks the team is over its head on this one, that the members are not capable enough, and that the situation is too serious to be left up to the team. Ballard thinks management should be brought in right away. He carries on for some time. Only after the most determined resistance from the team and the facilitator does Ballard back off.

9:30 a.m.: The engineers call a meeting with the team. The circuit boards are failing one particular test sequence. And that test sequence is associated with a specific transistor chip from a specific vendor that is on all the boards. During the discussion, the team members realize that the chip the engineers are talking about is from a new vendor. Why, just the other day they had to change out their bench stock to replace the chip they had been using with one from the new vendor. The team wonders if the new chip itself is bad.

9:40 a.m.: The team has located a few of the older chips that haven't yet been removed from the production module. Some of the new chips are replaced with the old chips, and those circuit boards do indeed pass the functional yield test. Clearly, the problem has been with the chip.

10:00 a.m.: The materials focal has put out what amounts to an "all points bulletin" and has located a supply of the older chips in another facility. The chips will be sent over immediately. The materials focal has also reviewed the problem with the materials department, which will deal with the vendor on an administrative level to have the defective chip fixed.

10:05 a.m.: The Daybreak team communicator rounds up all the Daybreak team members who were loaned out to the other team. The production module starts up again at full force.

12:45 p.m.: The Daybreak team completes the emergency turnaround order. The deadline is met with time to spare. Team members take a late lunch.

When I heard about the Daybreak team's victory, I was proud. I felt like we had finally re-created the spirit and effectiveness of Brandt's pick-up team that had inspired this whole Unmanagement adventure several years earlier.

I felt, too, that the Daybreak team had just demonstrated the power of Unmanagement beyond doubt. From the very beginning, the Daybreak team had monitored its own efficiencies by adjusting its manpower appropriately and had successfully overcome a serious challenge by using its own problem-solving skills and making its own contacts to other appropriate resources within the plant. At no time, other than alerting its facilitator on an "FYI" basis, had the team found it necessary to rely on management. Outside of the flap brought on by Ballard, the team's plan had worked flawlessly.

It showed me that the employees were well on their way to making the evolutionary transition that I've learned all employees have to go through when a company adopts Unmanagement. Remember the evolutionary progression that managers pass through? Well, the employee transition is a lot like it. It, too, has four stages, and each stage has its own set of identifying characteristics.

Evolution of Employee Development

Neanderthal	Traditional	Transitional	Future
• Fear	• No Trust	• Confusion	• Enthusiasm
• Politics	• No Direction	• Some Trust	• Trust
• Conflict	• Stress	• Some Innovation	• Innovation
• Bad Decisions	• Robot Reactions	• Questioning Poor Decisions	• Commitment
			• Continuous Improvement
"Ugh"	"It's just a job"	"Let me try"	"I can do it myself"

What Supervisors Worry About

I was high on life for a week after the Daybreak victory, and I'd just about convinced myself that the feeling would last forever when I was brought back to earth by an unexpected phone call from one of the plant's supervisors. I was in my office reviewing the plant's production figures when Henry Falder reached me. Falder, the supervisor of the Early Risers team, said that he and the other two supervisors on the first shift had a few things they wanted to talk over with me after work if I had the time.

"No problem," I said, "but could you give me some idea what we'll be talking about?"

"It's about our jobs," Falder replied.

"Your jobs?" I asked. "Is something wrong?"

"Well, to be honest," Falder said, "we're wondering if we're going to have any."

"In that case, Henry," I said, "I think we'd better meet right now. Come on over to my office."

During the meeting, the supervisors explained that with all the Unmanagement changes going on at FineFax, they were confused about what their role was supposed to be in the company. Worse still, they had even gotten to the point where they wondered if they had any role at all. As the discussion continued, it was apparent that what the supervisors were saying could be sorted into five main concerns:

1. By delegating their traditional responsibilities, supervisors will work themselves out of a job.

2. Team members will not be ready to take on the new responsibilities.

3. Team members will start to compete with supervisors and show them up.

4. Supervisors will lose the recognition they once enjoyed, as well as their authority.

5. Supervisors will be blamed for the mistakes team members make while they are learning how to handle their new responsibilities.

Now that was a real eye-opener. And they certainly did have a good point. Clearly, the role of the supervisor in Unmanagement needed extra attention. The new management style placed supervisors in a difficult position because they had to reconcile the demands of management coming down on them from above with the needs of the teams welling up from below.

In the days ahead, I met several more times with the supervisors, and together we worked out a program that clarified what supervisors could expect as Unmanagement unfolded. We agreed that there would always be a need for supervisors, but the nature of their role would change and fewer of them would be needed. Supervisors would henceforth be called "facilitators" to acknowledge the purpose of their new relationship with the teams. They were there to help the employees take on new responsibilities and make the transition to teams.

You will find that, in the beginning of Unmanagement, there will be little change in the number of supervisors involved, but as the teams become more proficient, they'll need less attention. Like many other companies, FineFax started out with a supervisory "span of control" of about one supervisor for every 10 people. Later on, though, that span of control broadened to one supervisor for every 50 people. You'll find that in the process, supervisors will shed their old ways of direct intervention in employee activities and become "facilitators," a kind of internal consultant helping the teams realize their fullest potential. They will no longer intervene directly, but will monitor various aspects of team activity such as business results, quality and scrap levels, training needs, and employee evaluations.

Our supervisors' transition program planned to deal with the need for fewer supervisors in two ways. First, when any supervisor left the company or retired, he or she would not be replaced. Second, supervisors could begin to prepare for other jobs within the company. Human resources would first interview them to help them match their interests with job opportunities, and then the supervisor could start getting on-the-job training through the Job Rotation program already in place. All in all, these arrangements corrected my earlier oversight.

I have to admit, however, that while some supervisors enthusiastically looked forward to their new opportunities within the company, not everyone was happy with this restructuring. A few people left for other jobs that honored their traditional role as "commander-in-charge." They were more comfortable in an authoritarian role than as a facilitator. Plus they liked the special perks that allowed them to be set apart from the rest of the staff. I guess at the time, I didn't fully realize all the ramifications of the changes I was making. This would come back to haunt me later, much later — but then, I'm getting ahead of myself here.

Chapter Eighteen

THE RATINGS GAME

A s your teams become more confident with their new working arrangements, the scope of their responsibilities will continue to broaden. In time, it may even include "Peer Review," a process that I think represents one of the highest expressions of employee independence and involvement. Let me explain.

In most companies — it was true in FineFax and maybe it's true in yours — employee performance reviews are one-on-one affairs between the employee and the employee's boss during which the employee basically sits in one spot and listens to the boss pontificate. As Unmanagement developed at FineFax, it became increasingly clear that employees reviewing other employees would always produce better results than traditional methods. There are several reasons why peer reviews are better than boss reviews:

- No one is better qualified to review a given employee's performance than his or her peers, the people who work side by side with that employee every day.

- The old way of reviewing an employee's performance was, in effect, telling the employee that it was important to please only one person — the *boss*. With Peer Reviews, on the other hand, the message comes across that it is essential to live up to the expectations of the entire work community, because all the people an employee works with are actually that employee's "internal customers."

- Performance reviews are a means toward self-improvement, and the more input, the more that self-improvement is likely to follow an accurate course.

- A boss would be well advised to give up employee performance reviews, not only because the employees can do it better, but also because reviews take up a lot of a boss's time — time that could be used more productively elsewhere.

The FineFax Peer Review process is based on the fundamental Unmanagement principle that employees are accountable not only for what they do, but also for how they do it. As a result, every Unmanagement Peer Review always has two essential parts: qualitative and quantitative. The qualitative part of the review measures performance in achieving the company's core values of quality, customer satisfaction, leadership, risk taking and innovation, and people development. The quantitative part measures performance in reaching the company's five chosen business objectives. Later on, we also found it made good sense to add a third part to the review process. The third part, which is unrated, is meant to help employees with their career development goals.

The Peer Review Evaluation Guide

To make the Peer Review process easier to follow, we created a Peer Review Evaluation Guide that organized the three parts of the process — qualitative, quantitative, and career development — into one short document.

Part I: Qualitative. The guide begins with a "Core Values" section that presents a list of the company's core values, a brief definition of each value, and several questions accompanying each value. The value-related questions form the basis for the evaluation of the employee's performance on any given value. For example, the core value of *teamwork* is defined as "the effective involvement of all employees within the organization in a way that best engages the individual talents of all employees." Then the employee is evaluated with three questions:

1. *How well does the individual listen to and respect fellow lemployees' opinions and ideas though they may be different?*

2. *How well is assistance voluntarily given to others?*

3. *How well does the individual communicate both written and oral information that contributes to achieving objectives within the team?*

Similarly, the core value of *risk taking and innovation* is defined as "creativity that leads to the development and implementation of beneficial change," and the questions that follow are:

1. *Does the individual learn from mistakes or try to hide them?*

2. *Does the individual challenge processes and try to make improvements?*

The responses to the questions can get any one of four possible scores: unsatisfactory, needs improvement, fully acceptable, or exceeds expectations.

Part II: Quantitative. The second section of the guide measures an employee's success in achieving the company's business objectives. It's very important to note here that, although employees work on teams, each employee still has individual performance responsibilities to help the team meet the overall objectives. When the Peer Review process first starts up (later these arrangements will be made between the team members themselves), the way in which each team member will contribute to the overall goals is agreed upon between the employee and the team's facilitator. At regularly scheduled times, the employee will go over his or her progress with the facilitator. They will compare the employee's actual results with the employee's preestablished target goals and analyze the cause of any differences.

For example, an employee may have a target of 2 percent of product rejected for quality defects at final inspection, but come in with an actual reject rate that is higher, say, 3.5 percent. Or the employee may have a target of 80 percent manufacturing efficiency and come in with an actual result of

82 percent. Of course, the employee is not downgraded in any way if actual results should turn out to be lower than the targets for reasons beyond the employee's control. For example, in this case the employee's reject rate was higher because new software was being used in the test equipment and caused a temporary aberration in test results.

The same system — ranging from "unsatisfactory" to "exceeds expectations" — used to score the core values section is also used to score the employee's performance in the business objectives part of the guide.

Part III. Career Development. The third and final section of the guide focuses on the employee's career plans. The career section is meant to help an employee identify and pursue specific career goals. It is not scored.

How to Implement Peer Reviews

Because the Peer Review process introduces several new concepts and techniques into the lives of managers and employees, you have to let it unfold gradually. At FineFax, for example, Peer Reviews developed through three stages.

Stage 1

- Employee completes self-appraisal

- Appraisal includes business objectives and values

- Employee practices with facilitator

- Outcome is not for the record

Employees complete the guides on their own and then meet individually with their team facilitator to go over self-appraisals. The discussions are meant to be informal. For example, an employee meeting with facilitator Henry Falder might say: "Henry, let me tell you how I've been doing in the last quarter. I've given myself top marks in quality because I haven't had a single defect. And I believe my interpersonal skills should get top marks as well. But I do see some improvements I can still make in keeping my work station organized. And, oh yes, I think I'm spending a little too much on tools, so I'll have to look into that."

The facilitator may agree wholeheartedly with the employee's self-appraisal, but the facilitator, always citing specific examples, might also point out other opportunities for improvement that the employee may have conveniently overlooked. Either way, their meeting has been a practice session only, and the results will not be included as part of the employee's record with the company.

Stage 2

- Anonymous written appraisals completed by other team members

- Appraisals are averaged by the facilitator

- Facilitator gives feedback to employee

- Outcome is not for the record

In the next phase of the transition to Peer Reviews, employees complete appraisal guides once each quarter for each of the other members on their team. These appraisals are done anonymously and turned in to the facilitator. The facilitator averages the appraisals and then meets with each employee. The facilitator tells the employee what his or her average scores are and then adds an important twist to the conversation, something like: "Well, Mary Sue, you did quite well on your willingness to cooperate with others, but it looks as though your score might have been even higher if it hadn't been for one low score. It looks as though somebody on the team doesn't think you're all that cooperative." This observation, although it seems inconsequential, is actually an important step in preparing the employee for the next stage in the performance review transition — the actual peer-to-peer review. The employee, hearing of that one low score, will naturally start wondering which team member turned it in. In time, the employee will no longer want the facilitator to translate the scores, but will want to hear the appraisals directly from peers.

Once again, the results of the employee-facilitator meeting at this stage do not count as part of the employee's company record. These quarterly updates are an important part of the overall Peer Review process because they give the employee a chance to correct potential problems before he or she meets with peers at the formal annual review session.

Stage 3

- Employee meets with peers
- Strengths/development are discussed
- Specific examples are given, not opinions
- Three levels of input are possible
- Annual meeting held on employee anniversary date

In the final stage, employees meet face-to-face with the other members of their team on the anniversary of their hiring date. The entire team, along with the team's facilitator, sits together at a table in a conference room. The employee who is being reviewed first presents his or her own self-appraisal, maybe something like: "My quality has been good. I've contributed to the decrease in scrap. I've made a lot of progress in my interpersonal skills. I think I still have trouble admitting mistakes, and I have to work on that." Then the employee tells the group what rating he or she should get, say, in this case, "fully acceptable."

Next, the other team members, using the evaluation guide, give their own assessment of the employee's performance over the past year, concluding with their own rating choice. Each team member gets five minutes to present an assessment and must be prepared to back up any constructive criticism with specific examples. The employee is not to contest the comments of team members.

It would be difficult to exaggerate the importance of this Peer Review session. Suffice it to say that the performance rating that gets the most votes will be included in that employee's corporate record and will determine his or her salary in the next year.

Originally at FineFax, the facilitator's evaluation accounted for 30 percent of an employee's rating score, but in time, as the teams became more sure of themselves, the facilitator's vote was worth no more and no less than that of any other team member. Naturally, you will want to make up your own schedule, matching ratings and salary increases, but here is the one we have been using:

Performance Ratings and Salary Increases

Rating	Increase
Exceeds Expectations	8%–10%
Fully Acceptable	5%–8%
Needs Improvement	2%–4%
Unsatisfactory	0%–1%

Supervisors and managers follow the same routine, except that their review process is slightly more involved because it can include two review sessions that encompass three levels of input — staff, peers, and senior management. We built this arrangement into the review process to tear down barriers between various departments and to emphasize the concept of internal customers. Early on in the FineFax review process, managers were even meeting with a senior manager, say, the plant manager, in a separate, third review session. But the whole affair got to be a little too cumbersome, and eventually the senior manager simply sat in on the Peer Review segment just as the supervisor sits in on the employee Peer Reviews.

Here Comes Treddle Again

Just about everyone in the plant regarded the success of the Daybreak team and the early development of the Peer Review process as signs that the fledgling Unmanagement program was now a secure way of life at FineFax.

I wasn't quite so certain. I knew that its long-term acceptance and growth within the company would ultimately rest on the approval of senior management. And although most senior managers could be expected to support the program based on the excellent business results it produced, there could still be threats from others who might challenge Unmanagement because it was new and unfamiliar and upset the status quo. In other words, there was still the problem of Walter Treddle.

And Treddle was becoming more and more troublesome.

During the Daybreak emergency, for example, Treddle had somehow learned that there was a crisis on the production line. Without calling me first, already a serious breach in the usual etiquette observed between managers, Treddle had simply walked in on the Daybreak team at the worst of times. Worse still, he was anything but helpful. Employees later recalled him saying on several occasions, "If we were doing things here the way we used to, this would never have happened."

Naturally, I was quickly called to the module to deal with Treddle.

"Walter," I said, "as you can see the concentration here is particularly intense at the moment. I'd like to suggest that it might be better for everyone involved if we got out of their way and, say, talked in my office for a while."

"That won't be necessary now," Treddle said. "I'm leaving anyway. I've seen enough. But you're right about one thing — we *will* have a meeting about this."

A few days passed, and I was hoping that after his aborted appearance on the production line during the Daybreak team emergency, Treddle would have calmed down and gone on to preoccupy himself with other business, but he had not. Instead, and true to his word, Treddle called me to a meeting at which he went ballistic and harangued me interminably about what he called the "disruptive effects" of Unmanagement.

I countered that business results were already improving noticeably and that employee morale was high. But Treddle insisted that the results were a "fluke" and that soon employees would long to return to the old ways they were used to. In fact, he claimed, he had even seen "uncertainty in their eyes" when he had come to the Daybreak production module that day.

Without actually saying so, Treddle made it clear that he would regard even the slightest sign that Unmanagement was hurting business as reason enough to scuttle the entire program.

Selling Senior Management

Although the Treddle meeting had been very stressful, I also felt that it had been extremely productive. For the first time I realized that every new Unmanagement program also had to include a plan to actively educate and lobby senior management for support. Clearly, if you can't beat the Treddles of this world outright, you can at least try to have enough supporters on your side to counteract their influence. The more contact there is between senior managers and employees who have experienced Unmanagement, the more chance you have of increasing management support for employee teams. The one thing that you don't want to do is distance senior management from Unmanagement. When you isolate senior management you create apprehension. Selling someone on a new idea is not an easy or fast process. Be prepared to go more than one round. To this end, I devised the following five strategies to win friends for Unmanagement.

1. **Build a business case.** Make a presentation to senior management that answers the basic question, "Why do we need Unmanagement and employee teams?" Focus on defining the concept and outlining business objectives. Show management the backup measurement systems that you have in place to ensure that the business is being monitored and looked after. They're probably the same measurement systems currently in place, but to show them again doesn't hurt. No one will do a better job of selling the Unmanagement concept than the employees themselves.

2. **Provide information.** Circulate magazine articles, books, and videos to senior managers to make them familiar with team concepts. This "seeding," as it's called, can prove invaluable. Some people believe it more if it's in print. Seeding also provides you with another opinion, because sometimes you can't be a prophet on your home turf.

3. **Update progress.** Invite senior managers to tour your facility. They can talk to employees themselves about how they like Unmanagement and how the business numbers have improved.

4. **Resolve problems.** When there are problems, bring senior managers in so they can see that employees have the skills to solve them. They can see the logical thought process and how people go about resolving conflict. They can watch the "tough stuff" firsthand.

5. **Celebrate successes and milestones.** Any time that you reach a new milestone, surpass a target, or have a success of any kind, invite senior managers to join the celebration. This will really give them an idea of the motivational powers of teams.

I put my plan into effect immediately and won a quick reward. One afternoon I found myself giving a tour of the team modules to Spencer Griffin, the senior vice president in charge of Comlinks' Western Region, who had heard about the Unmanagement experiment and had come to see for himself. Since the protocol attached to visits by senior level managers like Griffin required that he be accompanied by another manager of similar rank, none other than Walter Treddle himself was by his side.

After the tour was over, Griffin turned to Treddle and said, "Treddle, this is some very impressive stuff. I can't imagine what made you tell me that it wasn't worth my trip."

Treddle, who realized that some of his behind-the-scenes maneuverings had just been exposed by accident, looked quickly at me, then back to Griffin, and tried to make a quick recovery with, "Well, I, . . . ah . . . ah, I just meant you didn't have to drop everything and rush right down here."

Griffin, who obviously was unaware of Treddle's true feelings about Unmanagement, laughed as if we were all just a bunch of friends enjoying a good joke. "To the contrary," he said, "I'd like Trisha here and some of her people to come and talk with some of my people about Unmanagement. We're using teams a little, but frankly they don't seem to be doing very well. Do you think you can work her trip out for me?"

"Of course," Treddle said. "No problem." Although his voice sounded calm enough, I had been watching Treddle as he spoke, and a very peculiar expression came over his face, which reminded me of a person who had just swallowed something that wasn't quite fresh. And I realized that Treddle had just been rendered a little less "Terrible." He wasn't about to roll over and die, but at least now he had Griffin's influence to worry about.

"Life is good," I thought. "Life is good."

Relief from Treddle's stalkings may have been the most immediate benefit of my introduction to Spencer Griffin, but in terms of the theory and practice of Unmanagement, it wasn't the most important. I discovered that benefit two weeks later when Treddle, anxious to please Griffin, dispatched me as promised to visit one of Griffin's Western Region plants. When I got there, Griffin asked me to tour the facility and talk with employees at will, but on my own, because he was worried that if he walked around with me, it would make the occasion look too formal and the employees would be less relaxed.

I was impressed by what I saw. Griffin had indeed organized the plant into teams, and he had even discovered on his own that the composition of any given team was determined by who actually worked on a product. But the more I learned about the plant, the more uncomfortable I became. Something was not quite right here. Although the familiar team structure was being used, the teams themselves seemed to be drifting through the work day without a clear sense of purpose or direction.

At the end of the day when I sat down with Griffin to review what I had learned, I immediately asked him if the employees had been prepared for team life in any way. Had they, for example, gone through any training program comparable to Operation Egghead? Was management sharing information about the plant's business results with team members? And had management developed any programs to help break down the barriers between managers and employees?

"No," Griffin said. "We haven't done any of that. We just set up a few teams and let them do their thing."

In the conversation that followed, we not only identified the reason Griffin's teams were in trouble, but in the process we also unearthed one of the most important principles in all of Unmanagement. That principle, which I've subsequently seen confirmed time and again when I've visited other companies, goes like this:

Why Teams Fail

Too often managers create employee teams and then walk away from them, somehow expecting them to work wonders on their own. This is a huge mistake. Employee teams must grow out of, and be sustained by, a larger, overarching management concept that includes specific enabling policies, practices, and programs — especially company-wide employee education in business and interpersonal skills. Lacking such a connection, employee teams are like trees cut off from their roots and cannot survive.

Griffin listened carefully to what I had to say. He had risen from inventory clerk to his lofty management position by virtue of hard work and night school and one other ability — he was never too proud to ignore a good idea from anybody. In the weeks ahead, Griffin launched his own Operation Egghead and quickly became known as an enthusiastic champion of Unmanagement, second only to yours truly, of course.

Chapter Nineteen

HIGH QUALITY AND "FRANKLIN'S FOLLY"

I want to talk about quality next, but before I go any further, maybe now would be a good time to review FineFax's progress up to this point so we can keep things in perspective. You'll remember that, during my "Kansas" speech, I identified five areas within the company that needed improvement: leadership, process, people, quality, and customer service. Then I proposed that FineFax tackle them in order, one at a time, following six guidelines. In other words, improving the five areas was our strategy, and the guidelines were the tactics we would use to implement the strategy. Well, I'm pleased to say that so far our results seemed to show that we had successfully dealt with the first three of our main strategic areas: leadership, process, and people. Not only that, but along the way we had also discovered and added three new tactics to our list, which now included the following nine guidelines:

How to Unmanage

1. Identify and accept the need to change.
2. Realign corporate culture with vision statement and core values.
3. Develop specific business objectives and couple them to the vision and core values.
4. Tear down barriers between management and employees.
5. Make visual commitments to change.
6. Simplify production processes and redesign them with employee needs in mind.
7. Give employees all-encompassing training, not just skills training.
8. Share knowledge and decision-making.
9. Organize the work force into teams.

We had obviously embarked on quite an adventure, and we had already hit some rough terrain along the way, but we were definitely making progress. People were really feeling confident, and they wanted to keep the new Unmanagement program moving forward.

After watching the Daybreak team in action, I and the other Unmanagers were satisfied that the employee teams had built up enough momentum to move forward under their own power. So we turned our attention to the two remaining strategic areas: improving quality and customer service. We took on quality first.

When you reach this point in your own program, your first instinct will probably be to use traditional methods to improve quality, so I want to tell you right up front that there is a major distinction between the way Unmanagement goes about improving quality and the way traditional companies approach the same task.

By and large, traditional organizations take employees off the job and put them in artificial environments, otherwise known as "quality circles" or "quality improvement programs," and there they are asked to unleash their imagination and creativity in solving quality problems. But afterward the employees are sent back to an environment in which they are treated like employee robots again, where creativity and imagination are discouraged. And these organizations wonder why they have so much trouble improving quality.

Unmanagement, on the other hand, is based on the fundamental truth that there must be only one creative environment, constant and consistent, throughout the entire company.

When we got this difference straight in our heads, we were able to see that there are five critical steps to higher quality when you're using Unmanagement:

The Path to High-Quality Product

1. Establish a uniform quality standard and communicate it throughout the company.
2. Begin self-inspection by teaching employees how to measure their own quality results, as well as how to identify the causes of quality defects, so they can fix the defects themselves.
3. Organize employee team meetings to discuss quality.
4. Expand employee team meetings to include support services.
5. Make the transition from product quality to total facility quality management.

Since we wanted to get the 200 people on the production teams involved in the quality issue immediately, we designed a series of two-day training sessions — one session per week spread over the next three weeks. The first session would consider what's good and what's bad in product quality, the second session would explain how to measure quality, and the third session would teach how to go about fixing a quality problem once it has been spotted. During each two-day period, roughly 10 individual meetings were held so that all 200 employees could be trained in groups of 15–20 people to minimize disruptions to the plant's production schedule. At the same time, similar courses would be held for all the support functions, such as engineering and materials. Each training session would be taught by people from the quality control department with help from various facilitators and managers.

The program got off to a memorable start. I went along with the first group of employees, and when we arrived in the conference room for the training session, we found none other than Franklin Dell, the plant's senior quality inspector, standing by a long, narrow table on which were samples of the company's three fax models. Right next to Franklin was a flip chart with the following statement written in large letters on the first page:

> Productivity and quality are issues today because of the way companies are organized and managed and not because people don't know how to do the work.

Franklin felt this was a crucial statement to make at the beginning of any quality program. He wanted team members to know immediately that their personal integrity and ability were not being criticized, as is too often the case in the typical corporate harangue on quality.

Franklin greeted the group, and then an odd sort of grin came over his face as he said, "We're all here to talk about what makes for good and bad quality in our fax machines and, as you know, there can be a lot of different quality problems on the job, and we've got to know them all. But fortunately, there are some we won't have to spend much time talking about. For example . . ."

Right here, Franklin picked up a hammer and smashed the empty outside casing of one of the samples on the table. He smashed it vigorously; then he held the fractured fax aloft.

"For example, we all know that if we should ever see a product that looks like this, we've got a quality problem. Don't we now?"

The group howled approval. And Dwight Frasier, a team member known for his irrepressible wit, yelled out, "Well sure, Franklin, but I had one that looked that bad just the other day, and you quality people let it go through." And we all cracked up again.

The incident became so famous that in the future the busted-up fax was displayed at every quality meeting, affectionately titled "Franklin's Folly" like some important piece of modern art.

Now that Franklin had the audience in his grips, he had no trouble getting the members to follow him into the main body of his presentation. Together, Franklin and the rest of us used what was basically a "show-and-tell" format to rehearse what the standards were for good quality compared with defective and unacceptable product. As we went along, Franklin held up different samples of the fax machine to demonstrate what the defect actually looked like — here the soldering on the circuit board had failed to hold, and here the dialing buttons were seated wrong, and here the circuit board hadn't been screwed into the housing correctly. He finished up by displaying a specimen of the top-of-the-line model of the redoubtable FineFax fax, perfect in every way, on which he had tied a blue ribbon that bore the inscription, "Best Fax. Big Winner." When we left the meeting, we were each given our own copy of the newly revised and unified quality standard so we'd have it on the job if we needed it. Franklin himself couldn't have been more satisfied with the whole affair because as he had told me once before, he had been trying to get just such a program started for years.

The second week's two-day session took up the twin subjects of what should employees do by themselves to repair a quality defect after it has been spotted, and how should they measure and keep track of their quality results. Production team members had not had much experience in either area. For example, except in cases in which a screw had to be tightened or some other minor adjustment made, the employees had not been allowed to act on their own at all. Instead, they'd been told to wait for prior approval from either their supervisor or from someone in quality control. And, of course, while they waited, the production line continued to churn out more faxes with the same defect. Nor had the production teams ever been given any authority to measure their own productivity because that had all been done by the quality control department. And worse still, they'd been given little feedback about quality on the line.

Martha Reynolds, one of Franklin's disciples from quality control, had been selected to teach this session. Martha was particularly well qualified because she'd taught high school math before hiring on with FineFax. She brought to the assignment the same conscientious technique she had once used in preparing her daily lesson plans at school. When the group I was with came into her conference room, we saw that Martha had plastered the walls with various signs and visual aids that she obviously intended to use as teaching aids. And sure enough, Martha began her course with a quick tour of her gallery, explaining that these signs, or some close variation of them, could and should be used by any business to measure quality correctly. One sign read:

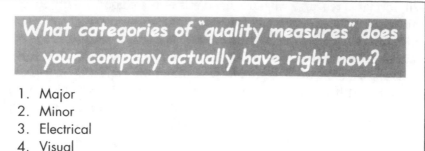

What categories of "quality measures" does your company actually have right now?

1. Major
2. Minor
3. Electrical
4. Visual
5. Mechanical
6. Other categories that vary for different customers

Another sign read:

What levels of quality inspection does your company have?

1. Quality process audit
2. Stockroom quality audit
3. Shipping quality audit
4. Out of box audit
   Do audit procedures ensure quality product or do informed, dedicated production employees?

And a third sign read:

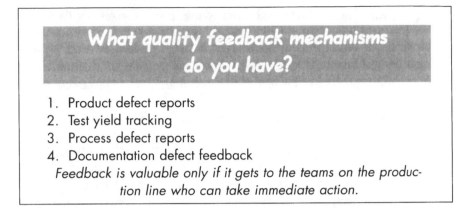

1. Product defect reports
2. Test yield tracking
3. Process defect reports
4. Documentation defect feedback
   Feedback is valuable only if it gets to the teams on the production line who can take immediate action.

All the signs, Martha said, pointed to the same conclusion: There could only be one measure of product quality — zero defects. And production team members must be given the authority to make that happen on their own. From here, Martha proceeded to explain how, in fact, we could achieve zero defects. There were three basic parts to the plan: measurement, interpretation, and action.

Martha first taught us how to use a basic graph to measure our quality results. Every day a team would enter a single dot on the graph composed of two figures — the total production of the previous day and the number of defects discovered in that production total. If, over time, the line connecting the dots should rise, that meant quality was getting worse; if it fell, quality was improving. Martha added a few embellishments of her own to keep the work interesting, such as her "nuclear disaster" quality level.

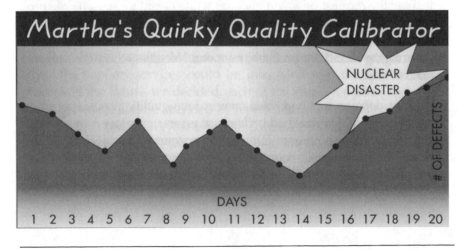

Since team members had to be able to interpret these results, they also had to maintain a list of just what kinds of quality defects had afflicted the previous day's work. Was it soldering? wiring? documentation errors? process errors? machine calibration? machine preventive maintenance? Each specific type had to be recorded. Each team had to elect one of its members to keep track of the facts and figures and to update the charts, which would also be on display in a team's information center.

Now, all the while Franklin and Martha were giving their training sessions, similar sessions were going on in all the other departments. Unlike the employee teams, the various support services did not have actual fax machines to inspect, but they did have other quality concerns unique to each area.

Engineering needed to improve its documentation, which, as presently written was practically impossible for the production department to understand. It needed to devise a system that ensured each report was checked thoroughly for readability before it was passed out. Human resources people, who always complained that they couldn't measure quality, routinely had merit reviews that weren't turned in on time. They needed to work on talking to the people who didn't file these reports promptly and randomly checking those people throughout the year to see that the problem had improved.

Probably one of the more colorful quality stories I like to tell involves customer service. I remember once that a customer was trying to get through to the customer service department to no avail, so she called me. After trying to call the department myself, only to hear the phone ring and ring, I put the receiver down on my desk while I went to check on the problem. Sure enough, when I entered the department, there had been an overflow of calls and not enough people to handle them. I could hear several phones ringing including, probably, my own. Needless to say, the problem was short-lived.

Other departments had their own unique quality issues, specific to the tasks at hand. Materials had cycle count errors, inventory forecast inaccuracy, and missing shipments. Information systems had projects past their deadline, endless rewrites, countless system changes, and so forth. It was easy to determine the quality issues that the departments faced, just by paying attention to the situations employees complained about the most.

At this point, Martha proposed an innovation that would turn out to be a big help to the overall FineFax quality campaign, and I recommend it highly. She said that each week, and even daily if quality problems were particularly troublesome, the members of each team should meet together to get at the "root cause" of their quality problems so they could determine what corrective actions to take.

During her class, Martha actually had us simulate a few of these "Root Cause" meetings to get the feel of them. For example, during one simulation in which we tried to find out why so many wrong parts were being put into one of the fax models, our questions included "Is it just laziness? Is there a process problem here? Do we have so many parts that look alike that we're getting them mixed up? And what about our bins at our work stations, are they set up right?" Much later on, as the Unmanagement program unfolded, team members would learn even more sophisticated techniques to get at the root cause, such as Pareto analysis.

Root Cause meetings were essential to quality improvement because they encouraged employees' ideas and sense of personal ownership in correcting the problem. And there was yet another reason why they were so important, but this one takes a little explaining. Three of our departments — engineering, materials, and information systems, or what we like to call support services — were supposed to support the employee teams directly. But in the past, in the world of fiefdoms, true, effective cooperation between them and the production people had been minimal at best. However, with the arrival of Unmanagement, and particularly when quality was at stake, the time had clearly come for all four groups to work together.

Unfortunately, we didn't quite know how to make that happen. Which brings us to the other reason why Martha's innovation was so important. Her Root Cause meeting turned out to be the most fundamental moment when the support services could be integrated into the quality control process. In the future, we decided, each of the employee team Root Cause meetings would also be attended by representatives from some of the support services. And what's just as exciting, we later found that this one meeting actually prepared the way to the eventual integration of the entire plant.

Martha went on to tell us, however, that although the employee teams would be figuring out how to correct quality problems in cooperation with support services, the teams would be the only ones responsible for making the actual changes on the production line. What's more, if they noticed a problem while they were working, they no longer had to wait for a facilitator or someone from the support services to happen along; instead, they could act immediately on their own.

For example, if they noticed that wrong parts were being added at a work station earlier in the production process, they could simply walk up there and point it out. While the employee teams and support services were getting used to the new arrangement, the quality control department would still be doing random quality audits as a backup measure to ensure that self-inspection was proceeding smoothly. However, these backup audits would not be confined to product only; they would also audit process issues such as if the employees have the right tools and if they understand what their standards are telling them to do. Eventually, as the teams took over quality measurement and control entirely, the quality control department itself would be dissolved, and some of its members would join the employee teams while others would take jobs in the support services.

Martha concluded her two-day session by telling us that, although we'd have our hands full in the days ahead simply concentrating on product quality, there would soon come a time when we'd realize that quality was an idea that went far beyond the products themselves. Everyone in the company would one day have to make a big transition in his or her thinking to total facility quality management. Quality had to become a part of everything that was done in the company. Phones couldn't be left ringing on and on; the hot food in the cafeteria had to be hot, not lukewarm; and bathrooms had to be kept clean — to name just a few areas.

And to emphasize her point one last time, Martha had placed another of her visual aids right near the door so we couldn't miss it as we walked out of the conference room. It read:

> Quality has to be a mindset that informs everything a company
> does; it's not simply product driven.

Chapter Twenty

CUSTOMER SERVICE WAS NEVER LIKE THIS

O n several afternoons during those days when the quality sessions were under way and when I didn't have to be in class myself, I was holed up in my office with the door closed. I learned later that my reclusive behavior was a mystery of considerable interest throughout the plant. In fact, two managers even staged a seemingly casual conversation outside my door so they might hear even the smallest clue from inside my office. Afterward, they started telling people that I seemed to be talking to myself in there. They said that although they couldn't make out the sounds all that clearly, they were almost certain that one time I'd shouted, "And why shouldn't employees be allowed to talk to customers?"

So it was that rumors began to spread that I'd "gone off the reservation," an expression commonly used around the plant to mean that someone had lost his marbles — you know, gone bonkers. It was said that the pressures of "this Unmanagement thing" had gotten to be too much for me and that any day now I'd have to be carted off for a long rest in a tranquil country setting.

They were half-right.

I had lost it a little, but it wasn't from the pressures of the job. Not at all. It was actually the sorry state of the plant's customer service that had driven me into seclusion. I knew customer service was the last of the five areas we had targeted for improvement and that we'd have to tackle it next, but I also knew that the job would be a lot more difficult than most people imagined. During my "We're Not in Kansas Anymore" presentation, I had mentioned only that customer service was in a bad way, but I hadn't said just how bad nor had I described the actual circumstances that had tipped me off. And that's a story worth telling now. It happened one day early on when I was on my way to one of my plant interviews.

The Case of the Two Shipping Clerks

I was passing by the shipping dock and I heard two of the clerks arguing. They were so intent on their argument that they didn't notice me standing there. Little by little, to my utter amazement, I pieced together what had happened.

A shipment of facsimile machine circuit boards had been sent out to one of the plant's distributors. On the way, the truck got stuck in a sudden snowstorm. To free his truck, the driver put one of the boxes of circuit boards under a rear wheel for added traction.

One of the clerks argued that the circuit boards in that box had to be charged against the shipping department's customer service record because they arrived badly damaged. The other clerk, however, disagreed because the shipment had nevertheless arrived on time. When I finally interrupted, I asked how it was even possible to debate the issue since damaged goods were so clearly a customer service problem. But one of the clerks explained that the question wasn't so easily answered after all; about a year ago none other than corporate headquarters had changed the rules so that only late deliveries would be counted as customer service "hits."

Can you believe it? I mean, clearly corporate had stacked the deck, rigged the game, to make the company's overall customer service record look better. I promised myself right then that before too long, I would take the time to ponder the meaning of what I had just heard.

Which is exactly what I was doing in my office — pondering, trying to figure out how to improve the plant's customer service. When I finally emerged, I had in hand a little chart that I'd drawn up that I called "The Unmanager's Master Plan of Customer Service." It was my best shot at fixing customer service, and I was hoping that even if people thought I'd gone slightly mad, at least they'd see there was a method to it. The chart looked like this:

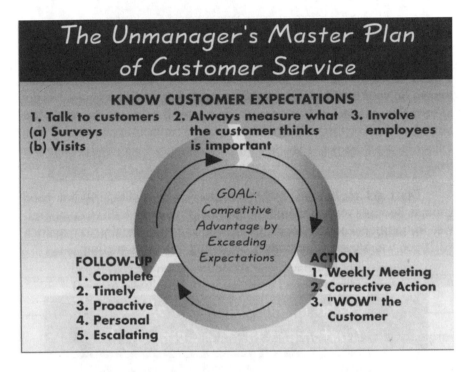

When I pieced this chart together, I started out with "Know customer expectations" because that's where I thought many customer service problems start. I can't overemphasize the importance of finding out who your customers are and what their expectations and needs are. If you don't do this at the very outset, you're likely to repeat a really serious mistake made by many traditional companies, namely:

Traditional organizations measure what they themselves feel comfortable measuring rather than measure what the customer thinks is important.

The story about the two shipping clerks is a classic example of point of view gone wrong. As far as the company was concerned, its customer service was flawless because the shipment had been delivered on time. But obviously that's not what mattered to this particular customer whose circuit board was run over by a truck.

If I could only give you one suggestion from what I've learned about customer service, it would be this:

> You must always measure customer service from the customer's point of view.

Unfortunately, most companies can't put themselves in their customers' shoes for one very simple reason — they don't talk to their customers. So your first step in revamping a customer service program has got to be making contact with customers. There are all kinds of ways to do that but, whenever you can, you should make these contacts in person and then follow them up with, say, written surveys. But, like I said, that's only your first step.

Don't get me wrong, making contact is good; it's just not good enough. Because, you see, there's another major problem with customer service in traditional organizations: Customer contact is usually very restricted. If you want to see what I mean, try taking this test sometime:

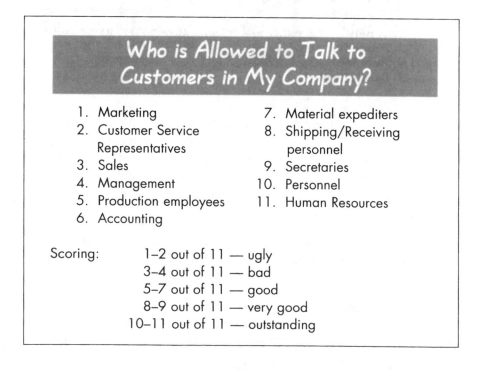

Who is Allowed to Talk to Customers in My Company?

1. Marketing
2. Customer Service Representatives
3. Sales
4. Management
5. Production employees
6. Accounting
7. Material expediters
8. Shipping/Receiving personnel
9. Secretaries
10. Personnel
11. Human Resources

Scoring:
- 1–2 out of 11 — ugly
- 3–4 out of 11 — bad
- 5–7 out of 11 — good
- 8–9 out of 11 — very good
- 10–11 out of 11 — outstanding

Don't feel too bad if you score only 3 out of 11 because that's exactly what you'll find in most companies — only sales, marketing, and customer service representatives (if there are any) are allowed to talk directly with customers. This is a big mistake.

Most often, companies will say that everyone beyond the select few is too busy with other concerns to get involved in customer service. I think this is a cop-out. These companies are simply afraid that anyone else — production employees in particular — will say something dumb that will offend the customer.

Unmanagement sees things differently:

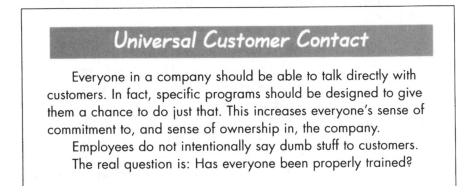

Universal Customer Contact

Everyone in a company should be able to talk directly with customers. In fact, specific programs should be designed to give them a chance to do just that. This increases everyone's sense of commitment to, and sense of ownership in, the company.
Employees do not intentionally say dumb stuff to customers. The real question is: Has everyone been properly trained?

As I tried to show in my diagram, once your customer service program is up and running, your success in meeting customers' expectations must be monitored constantly with a consistent program of action. At FineFax, for example, we have a weekly meeting attended by elected representatives from all the production and support service teams in the company. At this meeting, the reps will not only review past performance, but also devise appropriately extraordinary responses to customers with service complaints. And the emphasis is on "extraordinary." Actually, we call them "WOW" responses, and they might include personal letters of apology, instant refunds, or immediate replacements. In other words, we're doing whatever it takes to keep customers happy and make them say, "Wow!" I realize this whole "WOW" thing may sound a little dopey to you, but I've learned time and again that there's an excellent reason for it.

Recovery is extremely important because that's really what the customer will remember — not that you missed, but how you recovered.

Why "Wow" the Customer

If a company meets customers' expectations 100 percent of the time, that company will still only appear to be adequate in the customer's eyes because the company will only be doing what it said it would. The way to exceed customer expectations is to go one step further, and the only way you can do that is when you have a service mistake. When you have a service mistake, you've got to react in some extraordinary way that tells the customer that you realize there's been a mistake and that the customer is unhappy and that you're willing to do anything to make up for it.

In the last part of my chart, I wanted to get at the idea that just as there must be a specific action program, there must also be a well-organized follow-up plan to ensure that customer complaints are in fact being resolved. And that follow-up plan should always include some type of escalation strategy because there will always be customer service issues that will defy solution for whatever reason at the more grassroots levels of the company. Those issues should be able to find their way to the most senior Unmanager in the facility who will then make it his or her personal responsibility.

We put the Master Plan into practice immediately, and if the content of the plan was unconventional, so was its implementation. Since I believe that a company's senior Unmanagers should take the lead in establishing a customer service program, I convinced all of ours to spend a day on the phones surveying customers about their needs and expectations. We ran the program from the cafeteria just like a telethon. At one time or another, everybody in the plant must have stopped by to get a look at us Unmanagers working those phones. It was a riot and a spectacular visual commitment to change if there ever was one. It paid off in other ways, too. From the results of that telethon, we put together a list of standard measures to help track customer satisfaction.

Measuring Customer Satisfaction

1. On-time delivery (complete or incomplete)
2. Product does not work
3. Product damaged in transit
4. Product visually imperfect
5. Wrong product shipped
6. Wrong product ordered
7. Wrong packaging
8. Incorrect documentation

It may not look like such a big deal, but putting this list together was a major breakthrough for us. For the first time we were trying to measure service from the customer's point of view, and we were also sticking to a single yardstick rather than changing our measures to make ourselves look good.

Shortly after the Unmanagers' telethon, FineFax had its first plant-wide customer service meeting. In the future, it would be held at the same time every week, and it would be attended by elected representatives from all the teams in the facility. These representatives would, in turn, take reports back to their teammates.

The first half of that first meeting was spent explaining how the Master Plan itself worked and introducing the new customer service standards. In the second half, we went through the meeting agenda as it would be practiced at all future meetings.

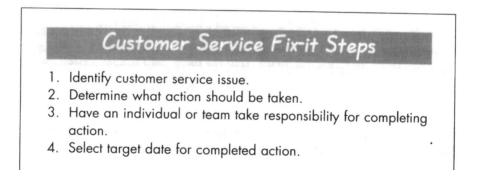

The Customer Service Meeting Agenda

1. All teams are represented.
2. The trend of all service issues is analyzed.
3. The number of new and repeat offenses is analyzed.
4. Root causes of new and repeat offenses are identified.
5. Specific actions to correct offenses and WOW the customer are assigned.
6. Progress reports on recoveries already under way are given by the individual or team responsible.

We also went through an example of how a specific customer complaint could be resolved. There were always four steps involved in the process:

Customer Service Fix-it Steps

1. Identify customer service issue.
2. Determine what action should be taken.
3. Have an individual or team take responsibility for completing action.
4. Select target date for completed action.

Then, to breathe a little life into how the steps would work in practice, Andrew Price, a production facilitator, described a recent experience. He said that several customers had told him that the boxes the faxes were being packed in were too flimsy and that the machines themselves were being damaged. It was clear, he said, that new boxes were needed. So first he worked with engineering to come up with a better design. Then he found an outside vendor to build the box by asking for bids from three or four different vendors. He then chose a target date when the new boxes would arrive so they could go through a prototype run on the production line before they were actually put in use throughout the facility.

I thought it was a good example. Obviously, the specific details of any given recovery plan will vary, but even so, Price's approach did show that the underlying method of solving the problem would remain the same.

As I had expected, the Master Plan caused quite a stir throughout FineFax, but after two weeks or so, the initial enthusiasm seemed to have gone a bit flat. Employees were attending the weekly meetings dutifully and practicing with simulated customer encounters, but it was clear that many had begun to wonder if they'd ever see the real thing. They were beginning to wonder if this plan, which they'd been told depended so heavily on getting employees involved in serving customers, was just a lot of talk.

It was then, right when everybody was getting so edgy, that I unveiled my coup de grace. I announced that on the following Monday there would be another one-day Customer Service Telethon. But this time the entire plant was invited. Everyone was asked to sign up to work the phones for half-hour time slots. And if there wasn't enough room for them at this particular telethon, not to worry, I said, because from now on a telethon would be held once each quarter, which meant that eventually everybody would get a chance.

As you can imagine, even though they were excited about it, a lot of people were also nervous about getting on the phones because they were afraid of screwing up somehow. Therefore, we held a short clinic in customer service etiquette ahead of time. It couldn't have lasted more than ten minutes, though, because we only had two basic guidelines that we wanted everybody to have. The first was a list of questions:

What Questions Do We Need to Ask to Find Out Customer Expectations?

1. How is our company servicing you?
2. Are our products arriving on time?
3. Are you satisfied with our service?
4. Are we courteous?
5. Do we answer the phone promptly?
6. Have you ever had a bad experience with us?
7. What more can we do?
8. What can we do better?

And the second was a straightforward suggestion to the effect that, "It's okay to say you don't know the answer to a customer's question if you promise to find out and call him or her back."

The telethon was a big hit. In fact, it worked out so well that the event quickly became a centerpiece of our new Unmanagement corporate culture and was henceforth known as "Dial-a-WOW Day." Some employees even arrived at future telethons wearing special T-shirts to celebrate the occasion, one of which, if I remember correctly, read: "You haven't lived till you've been WOWed."

Chapter Twenty-One

"OPERATION PIGGYBACK" AND THE COMPANY OF THE FUTURE

For a couple weeks after Dial-a-WOW Day, I must have been walking around the plant in a trance because whenever I thought about the changes we had made, I was convinced we had reached the ultimate, the last word in Unmanagement. Little did I know that despite all the work we'd done, FineFax had still reached only a temporary layover on the way to an even more profound and far-reaching transformation. But I was about to find out, and I got my first clue when I saw that the employees had reached a new level of self-confidence.

It happened one day during a plant tour I was giving for a manager visiting from another company. I noticed an unusual display hanging on a panel of the information center near the Daybreak team's module. There among the charts and graphs detailing the Daybreak team's performance was a painting about three feet wide by four feet tall, colorfully rendered and carefully framed and matted. The bottom half of the painting showed a cross-section of an underground scene in which a number of men and women were standing in what appeared to be a small, dark cave. From the cave, a winding path rose gradually upward to the surface. Along the path were other men and women making their way to the surface, following signs placed at intervals along the path. The signs read, "To Unmanagement." The scene aboveground contrasted sharply with the one below. A bright yellow sun was set in a light blue sky. Two white clouds floated by, just above three birds in flight. There was a building aboveground that had "The New FineFax" written on a plaque above the doorway. More people filled the doorway of the building. They were welcoming new arrivals who had just escaped from the dark, underground cave. Although it was obvious that the painting had not been drawn by a professional artist, the message of freedom newly acquired was unmistakable.

At the very bottom of the picture were two other items of note.

First, there was a kind of legend in three columns describing the team members' perception of the Unmanagement evolution they were passing through. The first column, titled "The Way We Were," included the following list: management dictates, poor peer relations, management isolated from production line, supervisor-led peer reviews, bells for breaks, and traditional work schedules. The next column, "Where We Are Today," read: peer/self-reviews, modules work their own business, flex breaks — no time bells, communication barriers eliminated, quality at the source, and "team" concept. The third and final column, "Where We Are Headed," included: endless opportunities, managerial training for operators, total involvement in expansion planning, increased customer contact, and team members involved in training.

The second item was in the lower right-hand corner. There each of the team members on the Daybreak team had signed the painting.

I was even more impressed when I learned later in the day that each one of the teams had worked up similar paintings. To me, these paintings said that employees had accepted Unmanagement in an especially personal way. No longer was Unmanagement coming at them as a suspicious influence outside their normal experience; instead, each individual had now internalized its values and goals and made them his or her own. They all had taken on a new sense of initiative and commitment.

It was at that moment, standing there in front of the Daybreak team's painting, I first sensed that a transformation much larger than anything I had anticipated was at work within FineFax. The appearance of a new self-confidence among the employees was a prelude to an even more sweeping event — the central organizational structure of FineFax, which had always organized activities around functional departments, was about to take on a new shape. It was about to organize itself around products.

This dramatic metamorphosis, which had been gathering force quietly in the background of daily plant activities, suddenly announced itself openly when Heather Walsh of the High Voltage team came up with her idea for a new product.

Heather was an interesting personality study. In high school, she had been captain of the football team cheerleaders, as well as an officer in both the science club and the ham radio operators club. To her classmates, she was a curious blend of talents and interests that they could never quite figure out — at once an energetic, good-looking school booster and a bit of a nerd, fond of high-tech tinkering. After she graduated, her parents didn't have enough money to send her to college, so Heather took a job at FineFax with the idea that she would save up some money to help finance her education.

Heather had noticed that the trays that fed documents into the fax machines had limitations. They were capable of automatically feeding 10 document pages or fewer into the machine, but if the operator attempted to fax more than 10 pages in one transmission, the pages sometimes overlapped one another. This made subsequent portions of the transmission difficult or impossible to read. Heather discovered that by realigning certain gears in the transport mechanism that carried the paper into the fax and by altering the dimensions of the document tray, the fax machine could transmit flawlessly as many as 30 pages during a single call.

After Heather described her invention to her teammates, I was invited to the High Voltage team module to hear a description of the new transport and tray. I thought it was a great idea, and I asked the team to make a presentation to the plant's senior Unmanagers as they had been trained to do during Operation Egghead.

To prepare for their presentation, the High Voltage team members began gathering information from each of the departments typically involved in bringing a new product to market. They started off with the engineers responsible for research and development. The engineers, to

Heather's obvious delight, approved the new design and agreed to help the team build a prototype for the new product, christened "The Organizer." While the prototype was under way, other team members dropped in on the sales and marketing and customer service departments to check out the market potential for "The Organizer." They were given a random sampling of customers to contact. Their survey turned up some important facts.

Some customers said that they faxed more than 10 pages in any given transmission only occasionally. They said that it would be nice to know such a tray was available, should their fax volume increase, but that they were not desperate to have it added as a permanent feature, particularly if it would increase the cost of the fax machine. Other customers who used their fax machines more heavily said that a tray with greater capacity and a smooth feed mechanism would be extremely useful and that it would be well worth a higher price on the fax machine.

Based on this evidence, which would be borne out by more extensive surveys later on, the High Voltage team decided that it would recommend that "The Organizer" be included as a permanent feature on the high-end fax machines used primarily by high-volume business users and as an optional feature on the low-end machines popular with occasional users. Finally, when the prototype was finished, the High Voltage team met with the materials and accounting departments to develop a preliminary schedule of production costs and future product pricing.

Up to this point, everything had gone smoothly; then the day of the presentation arrived, and suddenly the proceedings got more than a little tangled. As it turned out, the High Voltage team's part of the presentation was not even the main event, and it wasn't the members' fault. They were well prepared and did a good job, but they were upstaged by a wholly unexpected development. The other Unmanagers and I were all in the conference room congratulating the High Voltage team for an exceptional presentation when Heather herself said, "Well, I'm really glad you all liked it because we want to make 'The Organizer' ourselves, and we'd like you to tell us what we have to do next."

Given the circumstances, the question was entirely appropriate and hardly surprising. I remember that at first all the Unmanagers in that room responded accordingly, looking at one another with expressions of self-assurance and control meant to say that at any second they fully expected one of their colleagues to explain what was a very simple plan of action.

And still we went on looking at each other expectantly. As each second passed, you could see our confidence begin to wilt, and without even saying so, everyone in that room realized that no one really had an answer. A simple question had suddenly opened up a black hole of uncertainty.

I was the first one to break the embarrassing silence. "Hey, c'mon," I said. "Let's not get too uptight here, okay? We just haven't thought this whole thing through yet, that's all. So let's work on it for a while right now."

A half-hour passed without any significant breakthrough, and the group grew more and more exasperated. The discussion had inched forward meaningfully several times, only to be beaten back each time by the same seemingly insurmountable obstacle. Everyone in the room realized that the successful launch of a new product required continuous interaction between the various functional departments such as marketing, materials, and engineering; and the Unmanagers well understood how the drill worked in a traditional management environment. But FineFax was no longer operating under the old rules. Now employee teams had to be included in the loop of interaction, and because we were straining too hard for the answer, the group simply couldn't see how to bring it off. We tried repeatedly to think up some model for an interface that would meld the teams and departments together. But the harder we tried, the more impossible the task appeared.

Finally, and speaking quietly as if the idea might not be fit to include in such high-level deliberations, Jane Lawler, one of Walsh's teammates, made an extraordinary observation.

"I don't know," she said, "I mean I'm not absolutely sure, but I think we've already got what we're looking for."

"What?" I said, jolted out of a mental rut. "What did you say?"

"Well," Jane said, "for a while now the teams have been meeting every week with the engineers and the quality people at the Root Cause quality meetings that we started after Egghead, and I don't see why we couldn't do the same thing for 'The Organizer,' only make the meetings a little bigger and add a few more people."

Once said, the truth of Lawler's observation was so immediately apparent that it had the percussive effect of a small bomb. The Root Cause meeting, of course; Martha Reynolds to the rescue.

We all realized that we'd gotten ourselves so worked up trying to solve the problem that we'd completely lost our bearings. It had taken Lawler to get us back to reality and a fresh perspective. Sure enough, using the Root Cause meeting as a model, we were now able to solve the production of "The Organizer." We called our new plan "Operation Piggyback."

The next day, one person was selected from each of the support service departments to assist the High Voltage team with "The Organizer." The roster included representatives from engineering, materials, marketing, customer service, and accounting — all of whom would normally be involved in a new product launch anyway. But this time, there was a radically different arrangement. In the days before Unmanagement, each person would have worked on a specific portion of the new product launch from within his or her own department. Representatives rarely met with their counterparts in other support service departments, and their direct contact with the employees actually doing the work was even less frequent. With Operation Piggyback, however, the selected representatives shared a common office on the edge of the production area close by the High Voltage team module. From there they worked on "The Organizer" exclusively. The arrangement created an active and continuous exchange of information between the support service people, as well as between the support service people and the High Voltage team. In effect and in practice, the support service representatives had become part of the High Voltage team. This new extended team structure became known as the "long team," to differentiate it from the "short team," another newly minted term that referred just to the production employee team members within any given module. The Organizer project, regarded primarily as an experimental production plan, was the only one of its kind in the plant. Since all the other modules followed normal production procedures, they were in effect carrying the project "piggyback" style, hence the name "Operation Piggyback."

By any standard, "The Organizer" turned out to be a very successful new product. It was popular as a stand-alone addition to existing fax machines, and it also increased sales of other FineFax models that offered the new tray as a standard feature. In its first full year, "The Organizer" was to increase FineFax revenues by almost $2 million.

But revenue was not the only benefit to flow from the new product; it wasn't even the most important. For the first time, the Unmanagers realized that it was not only possible, but also essential, to organize FineFax around products rather than functional areas as they had been doing all along. Using long teams and focusing on product had improved production in every way. Information flowed much more smoothly between the employee team and the support service people, and the Piggyback group was able to respond much faster to changes in the production schedule, as well as in the marketplace. At the same time, the new arrangement broke down more barriers, emphasized the importance of the internal customer concept, and gave everyone involved a heightened sense of ownership and commitment to the work.

In retrospect, the humble Root Cause meeting, with its early interaction between employee teams and a few departments, turned out to contain in embryonic form the critical genetic code for the complete transformation of FineFax's organizational structure. At the same time, Operation Piggyback had made it clear that FineFax had not yet reached an ultimate level of Unmanagement as I had thought; rather, it was evolving through four distinct stages of growth.

In Stage One, FineFax started out on its evolutionary journey organized like most other companies, basically running two largely separate organizations under the same roof. Both these organizations contained sev-

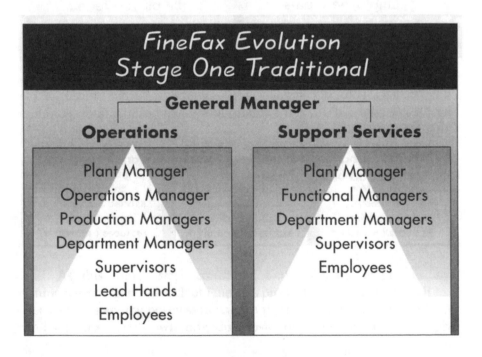

FineFax Evolution
Stage One Traditional

General Manager

Operations	Support Services
Plant Manager	Plant Manager
Operations Manager	Functional Managers
Production Managers	Department Managers
Department Managers	Supervisors
Supervisors	Employees
Lead Hands	
Employees	

eral layers of control identified by functional responsibility, and the whole thing was presided over by one general manager.

In Stage Two, FineFax adopted Unmanagement, established employee teams, and began to eliminate layers of control.

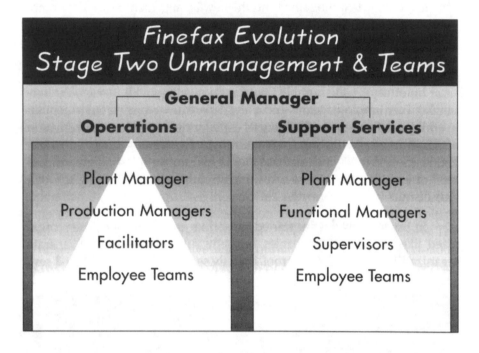

In Stage Three, Operation Piggyback introduced the concept of the long team and the idea that the organization could be built around product rather than function.

The fourth and most advanced stage would transform FineFax into a completely product-based company.

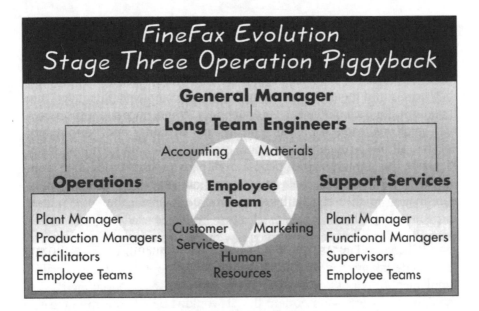

FineFax Evolution
Stage Three Operation Piggyback

General Manager

Long Team Engineers

Accounting   Materials

Operations

Plant Manager
Production Managers
Facilitators
Employee Teams

Employee Team

Customer   Marketing
Services
Human
Resources

Support Services

Plant Manager
Functional Managers
Supervisors
Employee Teams

FineFax Evolution
Stage Four Product Based.

General Managers

Product Line "A" Long Team	Product Line "B" Long Team	Product Line "C" Long Team
• Product Line Manager • Employee Teams • Materials • Engineering • Marketing • Customer Service • Accounting • Human Resources	• Product Line Manager • Employee Teams • Materials • Engineering • Marketing • Customer Service • Accounting • Human Resources	• Product Line Manager • Employee Teams • Materials • Engineering • Marketing • Customer Service • Accounting • Human Resources

As this fourth stage continued to unfold, the employees and Unmanagers organized each of FineFax's product lines to run as if each had been a free-standing business in its own right. Each product was produced and supported by its own individual roster of people, which included the employee teams that made the product, one or more people performing each of the necessary support service functions, and a product manager. There were no longer any separate and distinct support service departments at FineFax as there had been in the old days. Instead, the support service people and the employee teams had been completely integrated into long teams for each of FineFax's product lines. Where once support services and employee teams had held separate staff meetings and performance reviews, all these functions were now carried out within each long team. However, the support service people from each product-based long team did meet regularly with their counterparts on other long teams to make sure they were all using the latest and most effective techniques in their respective disciplines.

Changing FineFax over to a product-based organization was a complex undertaking, and the process would take about a year and a half to implement fully. But looking back, it's clear that it was important to go slow here. In fact, it was so important that it wouldn't be a bad idea to create a major rule:

Never Make Your Move Too Soon

Although the temptation will be great, resist moving to a product-based structure without first trying intermediate learning experiences like the Root Cause meeting and Operation Piggyback. People from different areas must be given a chance to learn how to work together. Otherwise, the transition to product-based long teams will be too abrupt, causing confusion and conflict.

How far you decide to go along this four-stage path of growth in your own company will depend on factors unique to your company. Maybe you'll find that things work just fine at Stage Two, and you'll decide to stay there. That's fine, you know, go with whatever works. Generally, though, I think it's safe to say that the more involved employees are in all aspects of creating their own product, the better off your company will be, which most likely means that you should probably try to go all the way.

An Unexpected Problem

I want to tell you, though, that no matter what level you've reached, sooner or later you're going to have to deal with an aspect of Unmanagement I haven't discussed yet — compensation. But if you read about it here first rather than stumble into it one day in your plant or office, you'll be a lot luckier than I was. Once again I was caught by surprise just as I was congratulating myself for what we had already done.

This time it was after work on a Friday afternoon, about a month after Operation Piggyback had gotten under way. I was in the conference room with the High Voltage team and senior Unmanagers to review the progress of Piggyback. The whole program was going along so well, though, that the meeting quickly turned into a mutual admiration society. I'd say something like, "You support service people are doing a fabulous job," to which the support service people would immediately answer, "We couldn't have done it without your help." Then I'd say, "But I really didn't have very much to do because the High Voltage team was just great." And the meeting went on like this for a while until a small, quiet voice somehow found an opening amid the self-congratulatory excess saying, "Well, I'm not really sure about this. I mean, I guess we're doing all right, but I can't help thinking that if people do more work, they should get paid more, too."

Wouldn't you know it was Heather Walsh. The same Heather Walsh who had brought the first Organizer meeting to a dead stop.

"What, Heather?" I asked, now looking at Walsh and still half-laughing at a little joke I'd just made to an Unmanager. "What was that you said?"

"I said that if you ask more of people, and you give them more responsibilities, then I think it only makes sense that they should get paid more, too. And that's not just for my team. It includes everybody on every team in the place."

And with this, we all started looking at one another, expecting one of our colleagues to respond. And after things went on like this for a while, everyone in the room realized that no one knew what to say.

"Oh, no," I thought. "Here we go again."

Compared to our first meeting about "The Organizer," the discussion that now began turned out to be a marathon. Although everyone agreed that Heather's observation was correct, no one was certain how to put it into practice. We spent the next five hours figuring it out, with a break for four large pizzas. But our deliberations did produce a preliminary plan for changing compensation at FineFax. We're still working on this part of our Unmanagement program, but I hope you can see where we're trying to go by reading these notes that I took at the meeting.

Meeting Notes

From: Piggyback long team meeting

Attendees: High Voltage team and senior Unmanager staff

Subject: Compensation

It was agreed that recent changes to the operations and organization of FineFax have significantly increased the responsibilities and workload of employees, and that consequently, ways must be found to increase their compensation. After a lengthy discussion of the issue, the group developed the following plan. In addition to the normal increases in salary provided for in the performance reviews, employees should be able to receive additional compensation in three ways:

1. *Development pay for new skills.*

2. *Immediate gainsharing in quarterly profits.*

3. *Long-term participation in profitability.*

Development Pay

In the typical corporation, employees are given pay increases when they are promoted vertically within their own disciplines or functions. For example, the base salary of an employee working in the production area will increase by a certain percentage as the employee is promoted to facilitator and then to product line manager.

We believe that employees must also be compensated as they increase their skills horizontally. For example, to become a senior Unmanager, an employee will need experience (through the Job Rotation program) in areas such as engineering, production, and customer service. Each new skill the employee acquires by training later-ally should also be acknowledged by a specific percentage increase in the employee's base salary. Initially, we might try an increase of 5 per-cent.

We feel this new arrangement will reward initiative and encour-age employees to become more valuable to the company and to them-selves.

Immediate Gainsharing

All employees should share in the profits of the company, and this should be done through quarterly bonuses so that employees get immediate feedback for a job well done.

Every quarter, financial targets will be set for the business. If those targets are exceeded, then all employees will share in the differ-ence between the actual results and the targeted results. The follow-ing is an example of gainsharing.

FIRST QUARTER TARGETS

Profitability	$250,000
Input Volume	500,000 units
Output Productivity	450,000 units
Quality	95%
Uptime	96%
Scrap	500 units

FIRST QUARTER ACTUAL

Profitability	$350,000
Input Volume	525,000 units
Output Productivity	500,000 units
Quality	96%
Uptime	98%
Scrap	250 units

Given this level of performance, $100,000 will be available for dis-tribution. We propose that the amount be divided equally among all of FineFax's 400 employees, which will give them each a bonus in this quarter of $250. In designing this gainsharing plan, we have followed what we believe are two critical rules:

1. *The plan should be kept simple, and it should focus on net profits.*

2. *The gainsharing formula should be the same for the entire company, as opposed to several different schedules for, say, the employee teams.*

Long-Term Participation

We all believe that in the near future, employees should be given a way to participate meaningfully in the long-term success of the company in addition to sharing in its quarterly profitability. Such participation may well take the form of an employee stock option plan in which employee contributions will be matched by the company. This particular aspect of the overall compensation package would encourage a long-term commitment to FineFax and would also give employees the additional security of knowing they will be building savings for their retirement.

Now that we had made plans to add a new compensation program to our freshly redesigned organizational structure, our group felt like it was truly building a model for the company of the future. Gainsharing was even added as the 10th and final item on our list of tactical Unmanagement guidelines.

The Piggyback long team meeting ended on an exceptionally high note that night. There was only one small glitch.

As we were leaving for home, Heather stopped me in the parking lot and asked, "Trisha, when do you think we can start in on the new bonus program?"

"I'm not really sure about that," I said. "These kinds of changes will have to be cleared with Treddle. I've just got to find the right moment. But don't worry, I'll work on it."

Chapter Twenty-Two

MOMENTS OF TRUTH

B y now FineFax was approaching the end of its fiscal year. There had been so much work to do that hardly anyone had noticed the time had passed. But a new concern suddenly focused attention back to the calendar: Would FineFax achieve the five business objectives selected at the beginning of the year?

Although the teams had periodically measured various business indices, the measurements had not been pulled together into a form expressly designed to summarize the five objectives. Overall, business results appeared to have improved dramatically. However, they had not improved in one flawless, rising curve. There had been moments of great success, such as the Daybreak team's early victory, but there had also been times when productivity declined as the teams learned to work with a new technique. As a result, FineFax was a little uncertain about how the business indices would sort themselves out.

Hoping to avoid any last-minute surprises, I developed a plan to have all the relevant figures available and in proper order for the final end-of-year accounting. I thought it was a smart move; unfortunately, it was doomed from the start and for reasons I couldn't control. I had already started assembling data with the accounting department when I was shocked to learn that a formal analysis of FineFax's business results would be done immediately. Even more disturbing, though, was the way I got the news.

On a Friday night, I was working late in my office. Dave Ballard, the plant's production manager, came in and asked if he could talk with me for a minute. Ballard didn't even wait for a reply and pulled a chair over to my desk.

"Trisha," he said, "I think you should know that the corporate audit team is going to show up here on Monday morning for a surprise audit of the plant."

I was stunned. "How do you know that?" I asked.

Dave sat there for long moment biting his lower lip every now and then.

"Walter Treddle told me."

I said, "But how . . . why did Walter tell you that?" And simultaneously, I suddenly knew, all in one piece, how it was that Treddle always seemed to know, and so quickly, what was going on inside the plant. Dave Ballard was the mole! I felt as though I'd been punched, and I slumped back in my chair.

"Well, you see," Dave said, "Walter asked me to call him from time to time to update him on the plant." He paused again. Finally, he said, "Trisha, I think I've made a big mistake." Then he went through an abbreviated version of his contacts with Treddle.

"You were misled," I said. "It really wasn't your fault. You didn't know what he was up to."

"I wish I didn't have to say this, Trisha," Dave said, "but that's not true. I knew he didn't like the new program and wanted to stop it, and I guess I hoped he would. I'm sorry."

For the next half hour, Dave and I talked candidly about what had caused him to become Treddle's eyes and ears in the plant. Dave said he had expected to get the general manager's job and resented me from the start. On top of that, he explained, not only had he never worked with a woman general manager, but also he had not thought women were cut out for the job in the first place. He was also upset when I began turning over management responsibilities to employees while at the same time eliminating various management privileges, such as reserved parking, a separate lunchroom, and even suits and ties. He had felt that he had worked hard to advance himself in the company and that he deserved all the perquisites of his position.

"So what happened to make you come in here today?" I asked.

"I've been wrong," he said. "I've been wrong about a lot of things. Since Unmanagement started here, FineFax has become a much better place to work; I finally saw that for myself when I saw what the Daybreak team did that day. After that I just couldn't stand the idea that even indirectly I might be part of bringing it down. Plus, Walter has gone too far this time."

"What do you mean 'too far'?"

"I mean he has seen the business getting better, and he doesn't want to believe it. So now he thinks we're probably cooking the books, and he's called in the auditors. Anyway, that's why I came in here to tell you about the audit and that's also why I'm turning in my resignation."

I refused to accept Dave's resignation. I told him that only part of Unmanagement was about making business better; another part was about making people better. I said that even though what he had done was very disappointing, the fact that he was willing to tell me the truth was a sign he was trying to change.

"But, Dave, I've got to tell you," I said, "the way I see it, you've let a lot of people down and you're going to have to make amends to them. Exactly how you do that, though, I leave up to you."

Over the weekend, I called people in accounting and other areas of the plant to find out if they should all come into the plant for an emergency session to pull the numbers together a little more. But, no, it wasn't necessary. The plant's numbers, they all agreed, were already sufficiently well organized to withstand the scrutiny of the corporate auditors. They really had only one concern — although they knew results had improved, they were not sure if they had improved enough to satisfy each of the business objectives to the last percentage point.

When the corporate audit team arrived Monday morning, I greeted them with the appropriate amount of surprise and then surprised them in turn. The audit team, I said, could investigate any area of the plant at any time. And although auditors were always accompanied by a plant's general manager, I said I was so sure that the auditors would not encounter any problems that I would stay behind in my office.

Three days later, the audit team had completed its work. Before they left, one of the auditors gave me a copy of the report they'd be turning in to both Treddle and the company's chief financial officer. For the most part, it was the standard document that audit teams always produced, but there was one unusual and, for me, glorious exception. The following addendum had been added to the routine descriptions and financial schedules.

The Audit Team's Addendum

To: Kenneth Parent, Vice President and Chief Financial Officer
        Walter Treddle, Vice President, Eastern Region

From: Corporate Audit

Subject: Addendum to audit review FineFax plant /Reg. 14z

Introduction

Nearly 11 months ago, the managers and employees of FineFax adopted a new approach to operating their business, which they call "Unmanagement." As documented elsewhere in this report, this new approach, although unconventional, has produced exceptional results measured by any and all standards routinely applied to Comlinks' business interests. However, the managers and employees have also selected five business objectives of their own design against which they intend to appraise the performance of the FineFax business. For this reason, the members of the audit team also made an informal evaluation of the plant according to these customized criteria. Although these criteria were meant to be applied against a full 12-month accounting period, and realizing that such a period has not yet passed, it appears certain nonetheless that barring some extraordinary business reversal, FineFax will meet or exceed each of its own performance targets. The following discussion is meant to identify those targets and to describe some of the ways they were attained. This information was developed from FineFax financial records and interviews with plant personnel at all levels.

1. Reduce operating costs by 20 percent

Under the new Unmanagement program, employees, now working in teams, are responsible for signing off on their scrap. The scrap rate has since declined by nearly 40 percent, which saved some $600,000 in operating costs. Similarly, the cost of various tools such as soldering guns, screwdrivers, gloves, and safety glasses — all items that are now budgeted and managed by the employee teams — was reduced by 50 percent. Changes brought about by the Unmanagement program have also produced savings in other areas of operating cost. For example, cycle time, quality, and yields have all improved; as a result, overtime hours have been reduced substantially.

Personnel has also produced another area of important savings. Since the Unmanagement program began, two managers and two supervisors either transferred to other jobs within Comlinks or were redeployed to other positions within FineFax itself. And because the employee teams are now responsible for their own quality control, FineFax has also eliminated the job designation "quality inspector." Employees in this job have likewise been assigned to other areas in the plant.

2. Reduce finished goods inventory by 30 percent

FineFax has reduced its finished goods inventory in two ways. First, employees have weeded out obsolete inventory. Although this resulted in one-time write-down, the write-down was more than offset by FineFax's second inventory reduction strategy. In that strategy, changes made to the FineFax production line have enabled the plant to get out more product more quickly. As a result, the plant now bases its inventory requirements on current demand rather than on the historical forecasting methods it had used in the past. Previously, the plant had maintained a large inventory of finished goods as a measure of protection against the unpredictability of customer demand and the longer lead times in adapting to shifts in that demand. Funds formerly invested in finished goods have been freed up for investment in raw materials that, in turn, has given the plant greater production flexibility.

It should also be noted that the employee teams are now responsible for counting their own inventory. Currently, plant managers expect that this particular innovation will create additional savings by eliminating the need to shut down the entire production line for the annual physical inventory count as in the past.

3. Improve manufacturing cycle time by 30 percent

Prior to Unmanagement, FineFax had used a single conventional production line. The production line has since been broken up into three so-called modules. The new arrangement has improved cycle time in several ways. First, staging areas between the various steps in the production process have been eliminated. Second, communication is much faster between members of the module teams, and they no longer lose production time waiting for management personnel to oversee production problems. Third, team members have started scheduling their own work, which has reduced their setup times. The materials department still supplies the teams with the overall volume requirements, but the teams are free to decide on the best way to run the total volume through the modules. Finally, the redesign of the production line has inspired numerous process improvements. For example, certain bench stock items are now allowed to remain in the modules, which has eliminated repeated trips to the stock room. In addition, team members have identified and eliminated redundant test procedures from the production line, which has also improved cycle time.

4. Reduce the number of quality defects by 35 percent

FineFax made quality control a priority that received the attention of the entire plant. The managers first developed a single, uniform quality standard to replace a confusing collection of measurements that often varied by both customer and product. Next, quality control was incorporated into a plant-wide training program. Finally, after everyone had been trained, the employee teams were then asked to take charge of their own quality control. Many of the people interviewed maintained that FineFax has perfected a new quality control device known in the plant by the code name "Franklin's Folly." The audit team, however, did not have time to observe this device in use.

5. Reduce the number of customer complaints by 35 percent

The most important single contributor to FineFax's impressive reduction in customer complaints appears to be the plant's new commitment to measure customer service effectiveness from the customer's point of view. Although this would seem self-evident, managers at FineFax argue persuasively that under current Comlinks practices, customer service is more often measured from the company's point of view. The plant's new commitment has inspired a remarkable day-long telethon event, called "Dial-a-WOW," during which employees personally contact customers.

As a final note, the audit team would like to point out that there appear to be several other benefits in addition to those outlined above. For example, the plant's safety statistics have improved some 25 percent because of the new module arrangement, which has streamlined employee movement within the modules. Other innovations such as flex time and the new four-day work week also appear to have heightened employee morale.

For about half an hour after I received the auditor's report, I couldn't leave my office. I'd read the report, put it down, get up and walk over to my conference table, look back to the report, and sit down to read it all over again. It was for me the single, most important document I'd ever received in my career. Not only did it confirm that FineFax had reached every one of its business objectives, but also it represented the first official corporate recognition of Unmanagement. When I regained my composure, I made copies of the report and personally put them on display in each of the production modules and in every department. At the bottom of the report, I wrote:

Congratulations.

Unmanagement is Unstoppable!

Gratefully,

Trisha Morris

Three weeks later, FineFax was featured on the front cover of the Comlinks corporate newsletter under a banner headline that announced: "Unmanagers in the Making: FineFax Scores Breakthrough with Employee Teams." And that was another major coup for the plant because the newsletter was distributed to all Comlinks plants throughout the world.

Chapter Twenty-Three

Good Times and a Parting Principle

J ust as the audit team had predicted, the formal year-end accounting confirmed FineFax's extraordinary results. As far as everybody in our plant was concerned, that meant it was party time. We rented the largest ballroom in the local hotel for an enthusiastic celebration of our own achievement.

On the Saturday night of the party, the room looked like a cross between a debutante party and a high school pep rally. Along both sides of the ballroom, the gilt-edged mirrors on the walls struggled to maintain their mannered elegance because this night they were decorated with variously colored felt banners proclaiming the names of each of the employee teams: Daybreak, High Voltage, Nighthawks, and all the others. A raised dais had been placed at the end of the room, and on the dais was a long dinner table fronted with a skirt of light-green bunting and reserved for honored guests. The table, like the mirrors, seemed suited to a gathering of diplomats, but clearly that was not the intent here. On the wall behind the table, a huge sign abandoned any sense of understated refinement with the bold announcement: *Unmanagement Rules!*

We'd taken to calling the event the "All-Plant, All-Purpose Unparty" in keeping with our plan to make the whole affair a bit different from the usual corporate ceremony. Just how different, though, became apparent after everyone had been seated. At most functions of this sort, representatives of senior management sit at the head table, but at the Unparty a representative from each of the employee teams sat there. Managers and facilitators sat with all the other FineFax employees at the tables, filling the rest of the grand ballroom. Among them, too, were several important guests. Kenneth Parent, the CFO of the entire company, was out there in the crowd and so was Spencer Griffin, the senior vice president of the Western Region, who had been an early supporter of Unmanagement. And, of course, their presence meant that Walter Treddle had to be there as well. Parent and Griffin, both of whom were certainly used to more privileged treatment, seemed to be enjoying themselves all the more for the lack of it. Only Treddle looked uncomfortable, unsure of his place. Whenever he caught the eye of Parent or Griffin, he smiled broadly, but when their attention moved on, Treddle seemed restlessly impatient.

Although the seating arrangement appeared to split the room into two separate camps — honored guests and everybody else — the design actually produced a lively and humorous dialogue that quickly involved the entire ballroom. The pattern was set even before dinner began as the various team representatives at the head table rose repeatedly to exchange toasts with their teammates. Then, after dinner, the dialogue grew increasingly louder and more energetic as the team representatives alternately bragged about their own teams and roasted the others. "I'd like to point out," said Mary Sue Dalton at one point, "that not only did the Daybreak team increase its own productivity by more than 20 percent, but we still had time left over to help the High Voltage team get its work out. What would they have ever done without us?" The remark drew long, theatrical moans from High Voltage and sharp hoots of approval from Daybreak.

Then, after the roast had just about run its course, a chant broke out somewhere in the back of the room and spread quickly to the front: "Trisha. Trisha. Trisha."

And that's when I came up to the dais to say a few words. But just as I got there someone hollered out, "Wait. Wait." And then I saw Dave Polanski and Ferlin Paige marching side by side up to the dais, one carrying a dozen roses and the other a small cardboard crown covered in gold foil resting on a purple pillow. I wanted to run but there was nowhere to go. Dave and Ferlin made a big deal of putting the crown on my head. They proclaimed me "Queen of Unmanagement," and the crowd went berserk. It seemed as though it took forever for the cheering to quiet down. Then I began a brief retrospective of how Unmanagement came to be at FineFax. It was a funny monologue for the most part, but at one point, when I recalled the type of manager I used to be, my voice broke just a bit and the room fell quiet. "I've learned a lot since then," I remember saying, "and you're the ones who taught me." The proceedings paused awkwardly for a moment until some FineFax wiseguy yelled out, "But wait till you see the bill."

After the laughter died down again, I said, "Now I'd like to introduce a man who let us try this great experiment. Without him, we simply couldn't have got it going. Give it up for . . . Walter Treddle." The crowd took up the call: "Treddle. Treddle. Treddle." For a while Treddle couldn't move, and he sat there at his place working his face into all kinds of astonishment.

Among other things, Treddle told the audience that Comlinks was well known throughout the world as an innovative corporation on the cutting edge of both technology and management. And he certainly was proud, yes, indeed, very proud, that FineFax was now carrying on this great tradition. "Oh, sure," Treddle said, "we've had a few differences along the way, but nothing major. Anyway, I want to tell you here tonight, that we'll all be seeing a lot more Unmanaging going on around here in the future."

From my table, I watched as Treddle returned to his. I saw both Parent and Griffin come over to him to congratulate him. At the same time, Dave Ballard, who was sitting next to me, said, "What made you do a thing like that, Trisha? I mean the guy was out to get you."

"Well, you heard what he said, didn't you, and right in front of his pals at that. I doubt Walter will be making trouble for us anymore."

"You believe that?"

"Yes, I really do. In fact, I think we may have just discovered another principle of Unmanagement."

"And what would that be?"

"How about … ah … yes … Strategic Humility. Yes, that sounds about right."

Just then, none other than Treddle himself walked over to my table.

"That was quite a surprise," he said. "And on top of that, royalty is a hard act to follow."

"I thought you did great, Walter," I said. "We all liked what you had to say."

Walter studied me for a moment as if testing a thought before letting it out.

"Well, I want you to know that I … I appreciate it."

"No problem, Walter," I said. "Say, by the way, I have this idea for a gainsharing program that I'd like to go over with you next week and I . . . ."

But before anything more could be said, Treddle and I were both startled by a sudden burst of coughing.

Dave, who had been listening in, had accidentally swallowed a large ice cube.

Chapter Twenty-Four

PASS IT ON

After that wonderful party, I didn't think things could get any better. Unmanagement had taken hold for good, and I almost felt like my job was done. Now, somehow, I would have to be reintegrated into the workforce along with my Unmanagers. Of course, things have a way of taking care of themselves, and it was no time at all before the mail started flowing in. Ever since the article in the company newsletter appeared, we were contacted by Comlinks subsidiaries around the world, all wanting more information on how they could implement Unmanagement in their own organizations. With the blessing of Kenneth Parent, CFO and VP, I was asked to put together a formal proposal about how to introduce a company to Unmanagement. Then I would personally tour our subsidiaries in several foreign countries and get them up and running.

Of course, my new job would mean a great deal of travel for at least the next year and, luckily, I was able to take my family with me. As a writer, my husband could pretty much work from anywhere, and the kids were looking forward to attending school abroad.

The first chance I got, I sat down to compose an Unmanagement presentation. What follows is a detailed proposal, to the best of my ability, showing how to implement the Ten Unmanagement Principles that I've mentioned as we've gone along. I have to say, now that I have it in writing in such an organized fashion, it's a lot easier to see how we were able to achieve as much as we did. I wish I had thought of this approach sooner, but then again, I didn't know what I was doing. And furthermore, I wouldn't have had as many adventures to share with you along the way.

So without further hesitation, here is your own Unmanagement Operating Plan.

FineFax, Inc.

PROPOSAL AND IMPLEMENTATION PLAN

Creating Unmanagement in Your Organization

Definition of Unmanagement

Unmanagement is an approach to running a business in which employees direct their own work because many of the responsibilities traditionally restricted to management have been shared with the entire employee population.

Principle

1

Unmanagement Principles

The Ten Principles You Need to Transform Your Organization

Identify and accept the need to change.

The leader of a business is the person who has to instigate change within an organization. Because of the leader's credibility and extensive knowledge, this person will instill the need for change with legitimacy. The leader does not command change, as much as he or she facilitates it. Employees, too, must take part in change from the very beginning, in order to ensure their ongoing commitment and "ownership" in the Unmanagement process. It is important to remember that change without ownership will ultimately fail.

Action Plan

1. Communicate your commitment to change to the entire organization personally.

2. Prepare to speak to your organization. In the presentation, outline the external factors forcing a change and link them to internal problems within your organization.

3. Describe the new direction your organization is taking and discuss how it will affect your process.

4. Ask for help.

Principle

2

Unmanagement Principles

The Ten Principles You Need to Transform Your Organization

Realign the corporate culture with a vision statement and core values.

Unmanagement requires both "hard" or quantifiable and measurable changes as well as "soft" changes that aren't quantifiable. These changes, instead, provide the company with the framework it needs to guide its future in ways that are less about ambition and control and more about empowerment and growth. Creating a vision statement is an excellent way to guide the overall aspirations of a company. Core values ensure that employees look beyond the bottom line for long-term improvements.

Action Plan

1. Create a vision statement that will focus your business, inspire a sense of ownership, and create a framework for problem solving.

2. Establish a set of core values that will provide both the company and its employees with a nonquantifiable, more value-driven approach to your business.

Principle

3

Unmanagement Principles

The Ten Principles You Need to Transform Your Organization

Develop specific business objectives and couple them to the vision and core values.

The vision statement and core values both address "quality" and how well a business should do. But you also need tactics or concrete business objectives to describe quantity and "what" a business should do. All are interrelated and create a constancy of purpose.

Defining business objectives can be difficult for new Unmanagers who are used to the old "fiefdom" mentality and are not used to defining their goals from a broader perspective. Creating objectives that provide the whole organization with realistic business targets is the first step in developing a team-wide approach to management.

Action Plan

1. Create business objectives that are both quantifiable and measurable.

2. Ensure that they can be linked back to the vision statement and core values by incorporating these "soft" values into your overall production goals.

Principle

4

Unmanagement Principles

The Ten Principles You Need to Transform Your Organization

Tear down barriers between management and employees.

The success of Unmanagement is largely dependent on management's ability to empower its workers. Creating teams, developing people, and instituting more sharing and caring policies all signify a new trend toward a more highly skilled and efficient workplace. Removing these barriers is also a crucial step toward instilling leadership that is focused on facilitating workers instead of controlling them.

Action Plan

1. *Practice what you preach.* Eliminate executive perks, institute a casual dress code, and remove any other physical signs of a management hierarchy within the organization.

2. *Admit mistakes.* Talking about human errors or a poor decision with employees opens the door for them to do the same.

3. *Allow disagreements.* Showing tolerance for different opinions is crucial to creating a workplace in which everyone is valued equally. It is important not to be critical. Instead, be collaborative and willing to work on a solution.

4. *Solicit ideas.* Ask for suggestions from employees and show that you value others' input.

5. *Take action.* To encourage others to offer what might be valuable feedback, always show you take suggestions seriously by following through on those that have been fully approved.

Principle

5

Unmanagement Principles

The Ten Principles You Need to Transform Your Organization

Make visual commitments to change.

When creating a new management structure, it's important to show a cynical organization that management is truly willing to back up its words with actions. Communicating your company's desire for change can be accomplished in many ways. At FineFax, we created several simple, cloth-covered folding panels that we called "Information Centers." We placed several charts on them that allowed employees to visually track each one of our main business objectives. We improved our physical environment and instituted policies immediately that showed employees we were serious about our dedication to Unmanagement. By demonstrating our commitment to a new management process at our company, we inspired others to commit to the new process, as well.

Action Plan

1. Review the changes you are making within your organization and determine any methods you can use to visually demonstrate these changes.

2. Implement the visual changes in an open and decisive manner, entrusting others to share in them as much as possible.

Principle

Unmanagement Principles

The Ten Principles You Need to Transform Your Organization

Simplify production processes and redesign them with employee needs in mind.

By reorganizing your production process to better reflect the needs of your employees, you can greatly improve feedback and communication that will, in turn, improve your product line. There are several rules to remember when creating process changes:

- Unmanagement facilitators need to involve employees in process changes and solicit their valuable input.

- People who are bonded together by both product and communication needs generally form effective process teams based on those relationships. Even in large plants, in which processes are spread out and teams can't work side-by-side, there should still be appropriate team communications techniques.

- All people in production processes should think of each other as internal customers and treat each other with the same high standards of workmanship and service they give to others outside the company.

Action Plan

1. Assess the production processes your company currently implements.

2. Work with fellow employees to simplify the production process and create teams that will meet communication and product needs.

3. Instill the team with the same sense of pride and respect for fellow team members that they accord to outside customers.

Principle

7

Unmanagement Principles

The Ten Principles You Need to Transform Your Organization

Give employees all-encompassing training, not just skills training.

By training employees in fundamental business principles and other aspects of your business, you are encouraging them to take more ownership in their work and in the company. It increases their understanding of how what they do affects the rest of the business and also makes them more valuable members of the organization. Such areas as interpersonal skills, hiring, presentation skills, and ethics and values help to make an individual a well-rounded and effective member of a team. Employee training need not be cost prohibitive; instead, as in other aspects of the Unmanagement process, training can be delegated to fellow workers.

Action Plan

1. Define what business training is necessary in your organization and develop a curriculum that can be instituted throughout the company.

2. Discuss the logistics of implementing training sessions for all employees. In some cases, classes can be taught during working hours; in others, employees may have to attend on weekends, for which they are paid overtime.

3. Include the costs for training as off-standard costs for 40 hours of formal classroom training per year, for a 2-year period. Cash outlays may be needed for all training that cannot or should not be accomplished in-house.

Principle
8

Unmanagement Principles

The Ten Principles You Need to Transform Your Organization

Share knowledge and decision making.

As employees increase their skills and understanding of business principles, they are more prepared to take on a larger role in the management of a business. Supervisors can facilitate this process by asking employees what they need to know and training them to undertake additional responsibilities. As teams grow to their full potential, the role of supervisors in an organization begins to change. Their traditional role as an authority figure is transformed into that of a facilitator, guiding teams to their fullest potential.

Action Plan

1. In order to determine what to teach people, ask them what they need to know. Ask employees which responsibilities they need to learn; then figure out a way to teach them.

2. As employees grow in their knowledge of the company and in their skills, allow them to provide greater input into the overall management of the company. Facilitate greater communication at all levels and encourage opportunities for fresh ideas and approaches.

Principle

9

Unmanagement Principles

The Ten Principles You Need to Transform Your Organization

Organize the workforce into teams.

Organizing your workforce into teams requires knowledge of how to function as a team and of the specifically defined roles to help members function within the team. Companies can ensure that the team process goes smoothly by sponsoring training sessions that develop team skills. In addition, it is important to set up a viable system for internal team structure. Teams need to develop at their own pace and to adjust according to their own problem-solving skills and resources.

Action Plan

1. Develop a company-wide team training program that will focus on the fundamentals needed in good teamwork, such as interpersonal skills, clearly defined roles and responsibilities, brainstorming, problem-solving techniques, and viable business objectives.

2. Create a mechanism for evaluating and measuring your teamwork, such as a team handbook, to ensure that it stays on track.

3. After creating your teams, focus on implementing an internal team structure to help teams take on their new responsibilities. To create this structure, try the following:

   - Define responsibilities.

   - Categorize responsibilities into similar functions.

   - Give each category a position and title.

- Ask team members to volunteer to fill a position.

- Rotate positions among members for varying lengths of time, depending on the complexity of the assignment, to maximize knowledge and experience.

- Make sure every team member fills each position at least once.

Principle

10

Unmanagement Principles

The Ten Principles You Need to Transform Your Organization

Establish gainsharing and other methods of compensation in addition to salary or hourly wage to reward and motivate employees.

As the responsibilities and knowledge of your workforce grow, so do the demands on it. In order to compensate workers fairly for their increased duties, it is important to institute a fair compensation program. In addition to normal salary increases for favorable performance reviews, employees should be entitled to development pay for new skills, gainsharing in quarterly profits, and long-term participation in profitability. Tying employee earnings to profit increases motivation and overall commitment to the company's objectives.

Action Plan

1. Develop a payment system that will reflect the new responsibilities and tasks that are inherent in Unmanagement.

2. Seek to reward employees for new skills that can enhance their long-term value to the company.

3. Ensure employee loyalty and commitment by instituting policies that tie earnings to profits. Make sure that the system allows for immediate feedback, rewards the whole company, and promotes financial security.

So there you have it. I have to admit, I have more than one reason for sharing my proposal with you. I guess I'm hoping you'll want to try Unmanagement for yourself. You see, I've got this theory that you only get to keep what you give away. As I see it, my job now is to pass on what we've learned here, in my official capacity as a representative of FineFax, Inc., and unofficially as a fellow business person and proud Unmanager who just can't keep a good thing to herself. I guess I'm hoping that you'll use some, if not all, of these techniques in your own organizations and that you'll be amazed at the results, as we were. Perhaps we'll even meet somewhere, along the way.

Until then, good-bye, good luck, and may your Treddles be few!